Day of Resurrection

Day of Resurrection

Leslie B. Flynn

BROADMAN PRESS
Nashville, Tennessee

To my in-laws
Anton and Lydia
Willie and Lucille
Richard and Shirley

© 1965 · Broadman Press
422-243

DEWEY DECIMAL CLASSIFICATION NUMBER: 232-97
Library of Congress catalog card number: 65-10339
Printed in the United States of America
6.JE64KSP

Preface

The most exciting day in the four Gospels is the first Easter. The empty tomb, the announcement by the angels, the perplexity of the disciples, then the electrifying appearances of the risen Lord to various persons make that "first day of the week" the most dramatic day of his entire ministry.

Five times he showed himself alive on that crowning day—to Mary Magdalene, then to loyal women, Peter, the Emmaus disciples, and finally to the apostles.

Who can fail to delight in the breathtaking events of that first Lord's Day? In a moment of testing Luther needed spiritual strength. Sitting fearfully in gloomy contemplation, he began to trace with his fingers on the table the words *vivit, vivit*. His despondence was dispelled and his flagging spirits revived by the message, "He lives, he lives!"

May our hearts be stirred by meditation on our Lord's several appearances that memorable Sunday.

Contents

1. The Empty Tomb 9

2. In the Garden 21

3. What Easter Should Do for You 31

4. A New Lease on Life 42

5. The Burning Heart 54

6. The Wounds of Christ 65

7. What Thomas Missed 76

8. If Christ Had Not Risen 86

to rise the third day, they felt his burial was the end.

The Women Wait

The nightmare of Friday led into the blackness of Saturday. The one on whom they had pinned their messianic hopes was entombed in a sepulcher. Reminiscing on his miracles only added to the disciples' grief. He who had made the deaf to hear, the blind to see, the lame to walk, the dead to rise, had been suddenly snuffed out by the combined power of religious leaders and Roman might. The one who had stilled Galilee's storm, chasing the winds back to their cavernous mountains, had died defenseless at the hands of executioners. They had supposed he would redeem Israel. Now he lay immobilized in the grave. The suddenness of those final events left them crushed. They had reached the end of the line. As Saturday came to a close, their despair deepened into black night.

The faithful women who had followed Jesus through his travels were likewise heartbroken. Watching their Master who, after cruel scourge and excruciating crucifixion, was taken hurriedly and laid in Joseph's unused tomb, these feminine followers determined to perform proper ministrations on the corpse. Denied opportunity on Saturday, since it was the sabbath, they spent a distraught day waiting for the first gleam of Sunday sky.

Very early on that first Easter morning silhouettes of a few women could be seen wending their weary way toward the sepulcher. The predawn gloom matched their mood. But beneath their almost inconsolable despondence were hearts of love, courage, and faith.

What love! Last at the cross and first at the tomb! What courage! To hope to enter a tomb sealed by Roman authority and guarded by Roman soldiers! And what faith! To roll away a huge, heavy stone! Many Palestinian tombs were hollowed out of rock, leaving a low doorway. Before the tomb was used, a large, circular stone, often over a ton in weight, rested at one side. After a body was interred the stone was rolled over the mouth, an adequate barrier against vandals. Because of its weight, this stone could be moved only by the combined efforts of several muscular men. To roll the stone from Lazarus' grave had taken more than one man (cf. John 11:41).

These women would have been unable to budge the stone an inch. To their bewilderment they found the stone rolled away and an angel standing guard who said, "He is not here: for he is risen, as he said. Come, see the place where the Lord lay" (Matt. 28:6). They looked into the empty tomb! Then they hurried to tell the disciples. At first their message sounded like an idle tale. The disciples ran to investigate. Several perplexing hours followed, ended by the Lord's appearance in the upper room. Finally, the truth gripped their unbelieving hearts! Tears turned to triumph! Sorrow into song! Jesus Christ was alive!

The empty tomb interpreted the disaster of the past few days and encouraged the prospect of a glorious future.

Amazing Discovery

Bad Friday ultimately gave way to Easter. The forces of evil must inevitably yield to the good. Tragedy must end in triumph. "Truth forever on the scaffold, wrong forever on the throne, . . . behind the dim unknown, standeth God within the shadow, keeping watch above his own." Paradoxically, tragedy often makes triumph possible. Had not Jesus died, he could never have risen. Peter wrote of the sufferings of Christ and the glory which should follow.

During the reign of Queen Mary I, a Christian, sentenced to die for his faith, morning, noon, and night the few days before his execution kept repeating the text, "We know that all things work together for good to them that love God" (Rom. 8:28). On his way to the scaffold he fell and broke his leg. He was ordered back to prison. While moaning in pain he was twitted by the jailer about his text. "Ah," the good man replied, "but it's true all the same. It's all working together for good!" Within a week Mary died and Elizabeth ascended the throne. The Christian prisoner was soon set free. His Easter came a few days after black Friday.

When Lazarus sickened and died his sisters puzzled at Jesus' delay in coming. But their dark day soon turned to victory when Jesus raised their brother from the dead. Someone said, "If it weren't for the night, we would never see the stars." Susan Coolidge phrased it:

> Lift up your heads, ye sorrowing ones,
> And be ye glad of heart,
> For Calvary and Easter Day,
> Earth's saddest day and gladdest day,
> Were just one day apart!

Years ago a tornado struck the prairies of Minnesota—killing many, injuring hundreds, and almost demolishing the town of Rochester. An elderly doctor and his two sons worked for days aiding the stricken—bandaging wounds and setting broken limbs. Their heroic work did not go unnoticed. Financial backing was offered for a large hospital, provided the doctor and his sons took charge. They agreed, opening in 1889 a clinic which soon attracted wide attention. For years from fifteen to thirty operations were performed daily. People came from all walks of life to the Mayo brothers' clinic. The Lord brought blessing out of disaster. William Cowper wrote:

> God moves in a mysterious way
> His wonders to perform;
> He plants His footsteps in the sea,
> And rides upon the storm.

Joseph thought it the end of the world the day his brothers sold him into bondage. Begging his brothers not to send him away from home and father, he must have cried out, "Is God on the throne? Has he forgotten me?" Years later when exalted to second ruler in Egypt, he was used to save many people's lives, including his father and brothers. He said to them, "Ye thought evil against me; but God meant it unto good" (Gen. 50:20). To paraphrase it, "You meant a black Friday, but God brought an Easter out of it."

Gloom must have enveloped the early church when its staunch deacon Stephen was stoned to death. Yet from that martyrdom flowed the rest of the book of Acts. The saints scattered through Judea and Samaria and preached the gospel everywhere. Paul, converted partially through Stephen's vibrant message, shining face, and forgiving spirit, proclaimed the Word to the end of the Roman world. The perspective of the years showed that defeat had been turned into victory.

> "Disappointment—His appointment,"
>   Change one letter, then I see
> That the thwarting of my purpose
>   Is God's better choice for me.
> His appointment must be blessing,
>   Tho' it may come in disguise,
> For the end from the beginning
>   Open to His wisdom lies.[1]

A missionary who fell into the hands of cannibals remarked, "Going to eat me, I presume?" The chief grunted. "Don't do it," said the missionary, "because you won't like me. I don't taste good." Thereupon he took a knife from his pocket and sliced a piece from the calf of his leg. This he handed to the chief, who took one bite and choked. The missionary worked on the island for fifty years. He had a cork leg. Little did he know that the tragedy which cost his limb years before would be used by God to give him entree among cannibals for half a century.

Orphaned at the age of five, Emmanuel Dannan was adopted by Samuel Norton and his wife a century ago in a little Wisconsin town. When he reached the age of eight he witnessed the murder of a peddler by his stepparents. The Nortons ordered him to lie to the police.

[1] Edith Lillian Young, "Disappointment — His Appointment," in James Gilchrist Lawson, *The Best Loved Religious Poems* (Westwood, N. J.: Fleming H. Revell, 1933), p. 97.

The boy refused. For his honesty he was beaten fatally, hanging by his wrists from the rafters of a crude log cabin. Cringing under repeated impact of willow switches, he sobbed, "Pa, I will not lie!" For killing Emmanuel, the Nortons served seven years in prison.

Sentiment ran high for the boy who would not lie. Citizens raised over a thousand dollars for a monument to the boy. A professional secretary was hired to tour the eastern states for more funds, but his expenses ironically totaled a thousand dollars. For over a hundred years Emmanuel's grave remained unmarked, but the people of nearby Montello, Wisconsin, did not forget. On May 2, 1954, two thousand people assembled to dedicate a handsome, six-foot, red granite monument by his grave. The inscription read, "Blessed are they which are persecuted for righteousness sake, for theirs is the kingdom of heaven." The people of Montello annually observe May 2 as Truth Day in his honor.[2]

In many cases we may never know the explanation of the black Fridays that cross our lives. Easter may be deferred till we reach heaven. Then the Master Planner will interpret. William Cowper tells of a woman whose life was ebbing away in almost unbearable pain. Her son, bending over her, said, "Mother, I can't understand why God should let you suffer so." Calmly she whispered,

> Blind unbelief is sure to err,
> And scan His work in vain;
> God is His own interpreter,
> And He will make it plain.

[2]*Coronet*, March, 1959, p. 53.

A Glorious Future Promised

The empty tomb proved Jesus everything he claimed to be. All authority now belonged to him. Rising from the dead proved his deity. He was "declared to be the Son of God with power . . . by the resurrection from the dead" (Rom. 1:4). No one would expect an ordinary man to return from the dead. But Jesus was extraordinary in his birth, teachings, miracles, death, and resurrection. His rising fits his supernatural character.

Others have claimed they would come back from the dead to communicate with the living. Houdini, the great magician and exposer of spiritualism, promised to contact his wife within seven years of his death. His wife acknowledged that he failed to get in touch with her. Clarence Darrow, who also disavowed spiritualism, good-naturedly promised a friend named Claude Noble that after death he would try to communicate with him. After Darrow's decease in 1938, Noble twice tried to contact him: first, on the anniversary of his death, March 13, 1939, in the Detroit hotel room where the pact had been made; second, a year later, when Noble stood on the arch over the lagoon in Jackson Park in Chicago into which Darrow's ashes had been strewn, chanting "Clarence Darrow, I am here in fulfilment of the promise we made each other. If you manifest your spirit to me, do it now." Both attempts failed.

Repeatedly Christ predicted he would come back from the dead bodily. His failure to rise would have annulled every claim he made to deity. When some years back reports spread that Buddha's bones had been discovered, the people of India lined the streets of Bom-

bay to pay homage. A missionary, noting their rever-
ential prostrations, commented to a fellow Christian
worker, "If they could find one bone of Jesus Christ,
Christianity would fall to pieces!"

In the eighteenth century two men of acknowledged
talents, persuaded that the Bible was an imposture,
determined to expose the cheat. Their strategy was to
attack what they considered the two bulwarks of Christianity—the resurrection of Christ and the conversion
of Paul. Lord Lyttelton, graduate of Eton and Oxford
and member of Parliament, who moved on intimate
terms with Bolingbroke, Pope, Chesterfield, and Dr.
Samuel Johnson, chose the conversion of Paul. His
friend, Gilbert West, took the resurrection of Christ.
Neither had read the New Testament, so each in fairness
to his assignment began to examine the evidence.

Both sat down to their respective tasks full of prejudice;
but the result of their separate attempts was that they were
both converted by their efforts to overthrow the truth of
Christianity. They came together not as they expected, to
exult over an imposture exposed to ridicule, but to lament
over their own folly, and to felicitate each other on their
joint conviction that the Bible was the Word of God. Their
able inquiries have furnished two of the most valuable
treatises in favor of revelation, one entitled "Observations on
the Conversion of St. Paul," and the other "Observations on
the Resurrection of Christ." (Lord Lyttelton on *The Conversion of St. Paul*, American Tract Society, 150 Nassau
St., New York.)

The empty tomb declared to the disciples that Christ
was victor over death. Death is a terrible enemy! It
plays no favorites, has a key to every secret chamber in

every nation, cares not for our plans, sometimes beckons the young before the old and the strong before the weak, but calls inevitably—an appointment all must keep. A hearse in Connecticut bore this ominous license plate, "U-2."

Christ through the gospel abolished the power of death (cf. 2 Tim. 1:10). Knowing its full power, he personally confronted death, determined to crush its grip. He permitted his body to become a corpse and to be buried in a sepulcher, but in every sense he overcame. Death, which leeringly had counted him its victim as he suffered for the sins of mankind, suddenly lost its power to hold him. Satan's cleverest wiles failed. Christ seized from the devil the keys of death. Angels rolled back the stone and then sat on it to show that death had been subdued. A new ejaculation broke the air, "He is risen!" He who had reinhabited his crucified body pealed out for all to hear, "I am he that liveth, and was dead; and, behold, I am alive for evermore, Amen; and have the keys of hell and of death" (Rev. 1:18). Though death may come to the believer, its sting has been removed. Some day its processes will be reversed as believers' bodies are raised.

The empty tomb gave the disciples boldness. In Gethsemane they had forsaken Jesus and fled. In the upper room they had shrunk behind closed doors. Suddenly cowardice changed to courage. A few weeks later they unflinchingly faced the same Sanhedrin which had condemned their Master, dauntlessly affirming, "We cannot but speak the things which we have seen and heard." Peter who had denied his Lord before one little maid, now before thousands fearlessly flings out the charge, "Ye have taken, and by wicked hands have crucified and slain" (Acts 2:23). Why the change? The next sentence gives the answer, "Whom God hath raised up." Then he adds, "Whereof we all are witnesses."

Their firm conviction in the resurrection accounts for their willingness to bravely suffer beatings, imprisonments, and the martyrdoms which ended most of their lives. They had seen one who had conquered death—who though placed as a corpse in a tomb had emerged triumphantly alive! They knew that Christ lived, and because he possessed the keys of death they too would live again!

The empty tomb illuminated their Friday tragedy, overcame their Saturday despair, and also provided them with a glorious prospect. As we experience our bad Fridays and black Saturdays, never let us forget that inevitably for the believer will come an Easter. Marie L. Olson has put it in verse:

> Before the blossoming of spring
>   Lies winter, bleak and cold;
> There must be stormy clouds and rain
>   Before the buds unfold.
>
> There must be showers in the sky
>   Before the rainbow's glow;
> There must be pruning of the vines
>   Before much fruit will grow.
>
> Before the resurrection morn
>   There stood dark Calvary,
> Before the glory came the Cross
>   With all its agony.

Thru death comes life, thru loss comes gain,
  Then trust, rejoice, and sing;
And labor on—ahead there lies
  With Christ, eternal Spring!

The resurrection changed bad Friday into Good Friday.

Instead of a lovely layout in a respectable casket hung
a bloodstained body impaled on a tree. When she saw
soldiers break the legs of the two thieves, she held her
breath, but sighed more easily when they left after
thrusting a spear into his side. Eagerly she watched the
body, helpless to rush out and rescue it. She puzzled
when noblemen Nicodemus and Joseph approached
the corpse. What were these Sanhedrinists about to
do? How relieved when they removed Jesus' body so
gently, anointed it, wrapped it in proper linen, and
deposited it in Joseph's tomb.

Those for whom much is done love much. Despite
attempts to link her with the sinner-woman of the city
(cf. Luke 7:37), no scriptural evidence paints Mary
Magdalene a woman of bad character or ill repute, even
though religious orders for reformed prostitutes are
called after her name. The ejection of seven demons indicates she had suffered a malady of severity. She must
have been an abject, pitiful sight before she met Christ.
Her entrance into the circle of believers was marked by
an exceptional miracle which made her a healed invalid,
not a rescued social derelict, henceforth to serve with un-
flagging devotion and undaunted bravery in the face
of dangers that broke the courage of the twelve.

First mention of Mary hints that she was well-to-do.
Ever wonder how Jesus financed his preaching tours?
One major source was funds donated by a band of
faithful women who must have possessed a fair meas-
ure of means. It was said of these followers, "Certain
women, which had been healed of evil spirits and infirm-
ities, Mary called Magdalene, out of whom went seven

devils, and Joanna the wife of Chuza Herod's steward, and Susanna, and many others, which ministered unto him of their substance" (Luke 8:2-3). The position of Mary's name as first in most references indicates her strength of affection.

> Who while apostles shrank, could dangers brave,
> Last at His cross, and earliest at His grave.

Sad at sunset, she turned away without a ray of comfort. The truth of the resurrection had not seeped into her heart as yet. Weepingly she walked toward home, symbol of despair for all who leave graves of loved ones. She had no hope of seeing him again.

How final death seems! So feared has death become that we try to avoid its mention by circumlocution. One religious group never uses the word *death*. Many speak of the terminally ill instead of the dying. Some may refer to funeral parlors as slumber rooms, while others may call the undertaker the grief therapist. We change coffins to caskets, hearses to professional cars, cemeteries to memorial parks, bodies to loved ones. But no matter how we dim the lights and rouge the cheeks, it's still death. One university psychologist, wishing to interview sick people on the subject of death, found his ambition thwarted by hospitals, large and small, whose professional personnel insisted that the one thing you never discuss with patients is death. What a radical change from the nineteenth century, when the processes of birth and reproduction were never mentioned in polite society; whereas, the processes of death were accepted themes of conversation, even of books. Today sex is discussed with minimal restraint, but a conspiracy seems to exist to keep silence on the details of death.

Time and time again death will come to loved ones and friends, forcing us to make that trip to the cemetery to lay them away with seeming finality. British archaeologists found the tomb of a little child in Egypt. In the darkness they lit a match to read the inscription which their guide translated, "Oh, my life, my love, my little one; how gladly I would have given myself to die instead of thee." The archaeologists removed their hats. Longfellow's "Resignation" says,

> There is no flock, however watched and tended,
>   But one dead lamb is there!
> There is no fireside, howsoe'er defended
>   But has one vacant chair!

Arriving home from the tomb, in the privacy of her grief Mary may have debated whether to have loved and lost was better than never to have loved at all. But she was to learn that best of all was to meet and love again. The grave was not finis. The gospel would write another chapter to turn despair into delight.

When the battle of Waterloo was in progress, all England waited for the result. Signals flashed from hill to hill by semaphore. The message read, "Wellington defeated." Sudden fog descended. News of the disaster spread like wildfire, spreading unspeakable pessimism. Suddenly the fog lifted. The rest of the message was received. "Wellington defeated the enemy!" Gloom gave way to exultation. When Jesus died, defeat overcame Mary Magdalene. But she was to discover that

God's message was not yet finished, for "earth's saddest day and earth's gladdest day were but one day apart." Sunset and sadness shifted into sunrise and gladness.

Sunrise and Gladness

Out of the mists that shrouded Joseph's garden that early morn shuffled a form, hesitating, red-eyed. Mary had arrived at the tomb a few minutes before with other women. Surprised at finding the stone rolled away, amazed at the angel's announcement, the women had fled frightened from the sepulcher—Mary hurrying to tell Peter and John, the others to alert the rest of the disciples. Peter and John had run to the tomb, scrutinized the graveclothes, and left. By this time the returning Mary reached the garden. Lowly hills were still enfolded by fog, as though reticent to reveal the crosses still standing. The aroma of flowers scented the air. Awakening birds plaintively broke the silence as the halting form stood bewildered, lingering and weeping. She was crying audibly, like a child, shedding tears.

The tears that have flowed, if gathered in one place, would make an ocean. Every century has seen its rivers of tears. In addition, countless broken hearts have suffered in silence, sighs without sobs. How many have wept alone, like Mary! The reason for hers? She had lost her Messiah, at least the sense of his presence. She wished to find his body, to anoint it. Perhaps at this moment unsympathetic hands were insulting his body, even casting it into the valley of Gehenna. She sobbed, "They have taken away my Lord, and I know not where they have laid him" (John 20:13).

A rustling made Mary look behind. Then follows the record of one of the most touching reunions in all of literature. She saw a form standing as if there for some time. But she didn't recognize him. Why did she fail to identify him? Was it the semidarkness? Was he standing in the shadow of a wall? Did her tears distort her vision? Was it the change in his appearance which caused everyone to fail to recognize him at first?

"Woman, why weepest thou? whom seekest thou?" (v. 15). These were the first words of the risen Christ. Though she failed to perceive who he was, he had been watching her all the while. Her tears did not go unnoticed. It was not strange that his initial postresurrection question should have been addressed to the drying of tears, since he had come to perform a work which would eventuate in the wiping away of all tears from the eyes of the redeemed. Future freedom from all sorrows was guaranteed by the opening conversation of the risen Christ.

Supposing him to be the gardener (for who else would have been there so early?) and still under the blinding domination of the idea that someone had removed her Master's body, Mary asked, "Sir, if [you] have borne him hence, tell me where thou hast laid him, and I will take him away" (John 20:15).

Jesus addressed her, "Mary!" A flash pierced her broken spirit. The call was so familiar! Voice and vision now blended! Instantly she knew him!

Turning completely around to face him, she exclaimed, "Master!" Was this the first sunrise service? C. Austin Miles has expressed Mary's thoughts.

I come to the garden alone,
  While the dew is still on the roses,
And the voice I hear, falling on my ear,
  The Son of God discloses.

He speaks, and the sound of His voice
  Is so sweet the birds hush their singing,
And the melody that He gave to me,
  Within my heart is ringing.[1]

Falling speechless at his feet, Mary reached out her hand to touch Jesus. He checked her show of affection. "Touch me not; for I am not yet ascended to my Father" (v. 17). He meant, "Don't expect to have my friendship on the same plane as before. I have entered a new phase of my ministry. I will not continue my work in a body on earth. After my ascension my Spirit will make his fellowship available to all believers everywhere at the same moment. I will be known henceforth after the spirit, not after the flesh."

She was to make known this truth to the brethren. "Go to my brethren, and say unto them, I ascend unto my Father, and your Father; and to my God, and your God" (v. 17). Obediently she hurried to tell the disciples that she had seen the Lord who had spoken these things to her.

Christ never appeared to Pilate, Herod, Annas, Caiaphas, the Pharisees, nor the Sadducess, but only to his insignificant, unlettered flock. More than that, the first one of his followers to behold him was a woman, and even more amazing, a former demoniac. Picture

[1]Words and music copyright 1940. Renewed by the Rodeheaver Company. Used by permission.

her less than three years previous—wild-eyed, hair dis-
ordered, foaming at the mouth, with long, sharp nails,
half-naked, screaming madwoman, avoided by people,
tormented by seven demons. Who then would have
thought that she would be the first person to see the
risen Lord? For the most unfortunate of people Christ
has superabounding grace and goodness in store.

Death for the believer is not an impasse. Rather, all
who, like Mary, receive him here and now will some
day meet him yonder on the other shore. An old Navajo
chief of the Southwest who heard the gospel repeatedly
from a missionary refused to accept Christ, claiming
"the Jesus road is good, but I have followed the old
Indian road all my life, and I will follow it to the end."
Some months later the old chief entered the shadow
of death. When the missionary came to call, he asked,
"Can I turn to the Jesus road now? My road stops here.
I have no path through the valley of death." But the
Christian's path leads to a meeting in the garden of
glory "just inside the eastern gate." Just as the Lord
spoke her name, "Mary," his own shall likewise hear
him call their name.

Apart from the message of Christ's victory, death
rings down the final curtain in the thinking and customs
of most people. One world traveler commented, "I
have seen burials in all parts of the globe. I have seen
Chinese bodies thrown out in the field for the hogs and
the dogs to eat. I have seen the Hindus in India take
their dead to the burning ghats. I have seen the Parsi
take the bodies of their dead to the roof of their temple
where the vultures swooped down upon them. I have

seen an African throw the body of his wife or child into a river. All of them did so without any hope of ever seeing their loved ones again. They sang no hymn of hope, but chanted only dirges of despair.

The early Christians, persecuted above ground in the Coliseum, were forced to pray below ground in the catacombs. Excavations near Rome have revealed some sixty catacombs in which have been traced six hundred miles of galleries, eight feet high and from three to five feet wide, containing on both sides several rows of long, low horizontal recesses, one above the other like berths on a boat, closed either by a marble slab or painted tiles. Both pagans and Christians buried their dead in these catacombs, but what a difference in epitaphs. Pagan inscriptions read like this:

Live for the present hour, since we are sure of nothing else.

I will lift my hands against the gods who took me away at the age of twenty, though I had done no harm.

Once I was not. Now I am not. I know nothing about it, and it is no concern of mine.

Traveler, curse me not as you pass, for I am in darkness and cannot answer.

When Christian graves were opened, skeletons revealed heads severed from the body, ribs broken, bones calcined from fire. Sample epitaphs vividly contrasted with heathen sentiments:

Here lies Marcia, put to rest in a dream of peace.

Lawrence to his sweetest son, borne away of angels.

Called away, he went in peace.

Victorious in peace and in Christ.

A father and a son had been shipwrecked. Together they clung to floating debris until the son was washed off and vanished from the father's sight. The father was rescued the next morning unconscious. Hours later he awoke in a fisherman's hut. He was lying in a warm, soft bed. In heartbroken agony he remembered his son! But as he turned his head, he saw his boy resting beside him. His heart leaped for joy!

One by one, followers of the Lord are swept away by the billows of time. But some day, awakening in resurrection splendor, all shall be together again.

3

What Easter Should Do for You

Be not afraid: go tell.
—Matthew 28:10

Modern custom camouflages the real Easter message. Standing at a Western Union counter just before Easter, a man noticed a list of thirty canned season's greetings with an invitation to check your choice. Samples read,

> From far away I wire to say,
> A very happy Easter Day.

> Here's hello from your Easter Bunny.
> May your day be bright and sunny.

> Easter's greetings across the miles.
> Here's to wish you a day of smiles.

Not one of the thirty conveyed the true significance of the day. Not a "Christ is risen" in the lot. The Easter bunny, the Easter lilies, Easter eggs, the Easter parade crowd out the real Easter message—that Jesus

Christ who died and was buried emerged alive, conqueror over death and victor over the grave.

After meeting Mary in the garden that first Easter morning, the Lord greeted the other women on their way to tell the disciples about the empty tomb: "All hail. And they came and held him by the feet, and worshipped him. Then said Jesus unto them, Be not afraid: go tell my brethren that they go into Galilee, and there shall they see me" (Matt. 28:9-10). Their lives were henceforth revolutionized. They now worshiped as never before. No longer did they need to fear. They had a thrilling message to communicate.

Once the truth of the resurrection grips one, his way of living will also be radically altered. For Easter compels worship, dispels fear, and propels one to witness.

Compel Worship

No human is worthy of man's worship. His knee should never bend to any finite creature, only to God. When Cornelius fell at Peter's feet to worship him, Peter ordered him, "Stand up; I myself also am a man" (Acts 10:26). Paul and Barnabas refused worship from the people of Lystra who because of their healing of a cripple thought them gods—Jupiter and Mercury. But when these women held Jesus by the feet in worship, and when later the eleven disciples seeing him at an appointed mountain in Galilee likewise worshiped, in neither case did he refuse their adoration.

Charles Lamb was discussing Shakespeare with a group of literary men. In effect, he said, "The difference between Shakespeare and Christ is this. If Shakespeare walked into this room, everyone would rise to admire him. But if Christ entered, all would fall at his feet in worship."

Jesus is called God in the New Testament (e.g., John 1:1). The Gospels picture him as possessing the attributes of deity, such as omnipresence and eternity. He performed the works of God: creating, sustaining the universe, forgiving sin, raising the dead. He made claims which placed him on an equality with God, asserting he was the Light of the world, the way and the truth, the resurrection and the life. Understanding full well the import of his statements, his countrymen tried to stone him because they charged, "Thou, being a man, makest thyself God" (John 10:33). But culminating, conclusive proof of his godship was his resurrection. Bursting the bands of death and breaking the bars of the grave proclaimed him the Son of God with power. Imagine someone sealed in a sepulcher on Friday, then on Sunday morning rising with power, rolling away the stone, appearing to loved ones, and walking miles! No wonder they worshiped him!

A little girl in China, taught at home to worship the idols on the shelf, learned at a mission station of Christ who died and rose the third day. Back home she took an idol into the back yard and buried it. On the third day she went to the spot, dug into the ground, and found the idol still buried. Going to her mother, she explained that the idols were worth only throwing away. She was henceforth going to worship the living Lord who had been able to rise from the dead! In a day when missionary enterprise operates on a two-way street, with Moslem prayer resounding in a Washington mosque five times a day, it is well to remember that no other founder of any religion rose from the dead. Mohammed is dead. Buddha is dead. Confucius is dead. But Christ lives!

At his own request King Charlemagne was buried in a sitting posture with royal robes of purple and ermine on him, crown on his head, scepter in his hand. When the tomb was later opened, the crown had tumbled from Charlemagne's bleached brow, his scepter had fallen into the dust from his lifeless grasp, his royal robes had crumpled in tatters about his decomposing form. His regal authority had dissolved in death. But one king, who was buried without any outward pomp or symbol of power, emerged victorious, lives today at the right hand of Almighty God, destined some day to rule this tortured world in righteousness.

So monumental was Christ's triumph that the day of worship changed. On the first day of the week the Corinthian Christians were told to lay aside their offerings, an order which Paul gave to all the churches (1 Cor. 16:1-2). On his stay in Troas public worship with sermon and the Lord's Supper was held on the first day of the week, even though Paul had been there seven full days, including the Jewish sabbath. Among others, an ancient document called the Epistle of Barnabas, penned in the early second century, bears this witness, "Wherefore we also celebrate with gladness the eighth day, whereon indeed Jesus rose from the dead." The first day of the week became "the Lord's Day." Churches today which are crowded only on

Easter should in reality be jammed every Sunday. All professed followers should join in *weekly* first-day worship of the triumphant Christ.

Robert W. Dale, pastor of a famous church in Birmingham, England, was preparing his thoroughly orthodox sermon for one Easter. In a new way it suddenly dawned on him that Jesus Christ was alive at that very moment. He kept repeating to himself, "He is alive NOW!" He entered the pulpit radiant and eager to lead the congregation in praise. Members of his church reported that thereafter every Sunday morning service, without fail, included the singing of an Easter hymn. Easter compels worship.

Dispel Fear

Fear "dogs" one's life from the cradle to the grave. The child is afraid of the dark, the youth of failure at college, the mother of losing her husband, the father that business may be bad.

Some fear is good. A healthy fear preserves against danger. How wise to fear germs, fires, speeding, rattlesnakes, and poison. A captain in *Moby Dick* said, "I will have no man on my boat who does not have a fear of whales."

But sometimes fear takes on high voltage and becomes destructive. Fear can cause paleness of skin, rapid heartbeat, shallow breathing, hoarse voice, or upset stomach. A lady in abnormal fear of germs remains inside her house, becoming a prisoner of her fear and forgetting that fear is ten times deadlier than germs. A great big fellow at the altar may be so terrified he cannot manipulate the ring onto the dainty bridal finger.

To the women that Easter morn, startled at meeting him, the risen Christ reassuringly said, "Fear not." Earlier that morning the angel at the tomb had calmed them, "Fear not ye" (Matt. 28:5). Later the ten in the upper room were to be saluted by Christ's coming through closed doors, standing in the midst of them and saying, "Peace be unto you" (Luke 24:36).

How significant that Christ's opening greeting to groups of his followers should be, "Fear not! Peace be unto you!" No fear of life lies outside his power to dispel, including apprehension at the past, unfortunate heredity, bad medical history, failure, unpleasant episodes, or wrongdoings. Our sins can be blotted out, put behind God's back, removed as far as east is from west, thrown into the depths of the sea, never to be remembered against us any more.

Likewise, Christ can dissipate fears of the future, involving possible illness, impending world disaster, old age, loneliness, and the unknown. A little girl on a train journey that crossed several rivers during the day shivered every time she saw water ahead. She didn't understand how these rivers could be crossed safely. But each time as they neared the river, somehow a bridge would appear to provide the way. After several crossings she leaned back with a sigh of relief, "Someone has put bridges for us all the way." So Christ who knows the end from the beginning has promised to make all things work out for our good and his glory.

Perhaps the most universal as well as the most intense fear is that of death. Francoise Sagan, famous French novelist-idol of French youth, who at nineteen years of age wrote a best seller, said in a magazine interview, "At times I wake up in the middle of the night and my hair stands on end when I think that I am going to die one day." During the Middle Ages the skull and cross-bones came into general use, carved on bridges, drinking cups, rings, and china as a constant reminder that life was fleeting. One philosopher, facing death, cried, "I'm taking a fearful leap in the dark." Evidence of the fear of death in our generation is shown by our obsession on youth, glorification of the body after death, and the conspiracy of silence on the subject.

A boy living in northern Idaho could never forget a timber buyer by the name of Benham who stopped for a week in the boy's home.[1] An outspoken atheist, Mr. Benham could recite with persuasiveness the main arguments of Robert G. Ingersoll. He frankly stated that he had spent most of his money and years proving God did not exist. Irrevocably he held there was no afterlife, neither heaven nor hell.

Twenty years later the boy, now grown into success-ful manhood, was attending a business convention in St. Paul, Minnesota, when his attention was drawn to a familiar-looking, gray-haired gentleman in the lobby. It was Mr. Benham. Though two decades had passed, he remembered the young man and invited him to lunch. Immediately it was evident the atheist had lost his poise. He acted like a man awaiting a death sentence.

Now seventy-one years of age, the gentleman ex-

[1]Sherman Rogers, "The Tragedy of Mr. Benham," *Christian Economics*, November 27, 1962.

plained that he was an incurable anemic and had less than a year to live. He then launched into an unforgettable story about an old lady who lay at death's door in a local hospital, where he had gone for a checkup. While there he had been conscripted by a nurse sent out by the dying woman to get three witnesses to a deathbed will which she could not sign due to a paralyzed arm. Entering the lady's room, he was struck by the utter serenity of this woman who had been bedridden for several years and who was now facing the end with a smiling countenance. The nurse rapidly wrote the whispered instructions of the stricken woman for the disposal of her property. When the three witnesses had signed the paper, the lady smiled, thanked them and said, "And now I am ready to leave this pain-wracked body to meet my Maker, my husband, my father, my mother, and all my friends who have gone before me. Won't that be wonderful?"

As Mr. Benham reached this point, tears started down his pale, wrinkled cheeks. "Look at me," he said in a hoarse whisper. "I've lain awake many nights since I learned my days were numbered, staring at the ceiling with nothing to look forward to except that my life would end in a handful of ashes. That's the difference between me, an atheist, and the lady I have described. She, believing, faces her final days with a smile. Here am I, nonbeliever, with every moment a nightmare, facing nothing but a cold tomb." He hesitated a few moments, then added, "I would shove my hands into a bed of red hot coals if by so doing I could secure a belief in a Supreme Being and an afterlife."

Death need not have any fear for the Christian, for the empty tomb points out Christ's victory over death and the grave. A little lad from a non-Christian family began attending Sunday school one Christmas time. He drank in the words of the teacher as the lessons advanced from the birth of the Saviour through his ministry and death. Often he begged his mother to come to church, but, possessed by a morbid fear of death, she refused, terrified lest the preacher say something about dying. Easter came, with the story of the risen Christ. After the lesson the little fellow rushed home with shining face. "Oh, Mother, you needn't be afraid of dying any more, for Jesus went right through the tomb and left a light behind him!" The grave need no longer be a gloomy vestibule but a friendly portal to heavenly rapture. Easter dispels fear.

Propel Witness

"Go tell my brethren that they go into Galilee, and there shall they see me" (Matt. 28:10), the Lord commanded these women. Whether he meant his flesh-and-blood stepbrothers or the disciples may be a moot question. Perhaps he included both, for his own brothers who had not believed up to now were convinced by the resurrection and joined the postascension group in the upper room.

What wonderful news! Could these women keep the message to themselves? On the contrary, the truth burned like fire in their hearts, impelling and propelling them to tell it out. Doubtless they ran, their feet leaping over the ground, their hearts singing excitedly, their voices exploding with praise, announcing to all who would hear that Christ had returned from the dead and would meet his followers in Galilee!

The early church could not contain this good news. To thousands on the day of Pentecost came the proclamation, "This Jesus hath God raised up, whereof we all are witnesses" (Acts 2:32). To the crowd on Solomon's porch after the healing of the lame man, to the Sanhedrin, to the Hellenistic congregations, to the people of Samaria, to the household of Cornelius, to synagogues all across Asia Minor, Europe, and right to Rome pealed the same thrilling evangel, "Christ rose from the dead the third day according to the Scriptures."

With time on his hands to think, one patient in a sanitarium, meditating on the transformation in the lives of the disciples from cowardice to courage, reached the conclusion that the only explanation was the resurrection of Christ. Only the miracle of the empty tomb could account for the dramatic change in their behavior. So strongly did they believe that nothing short of death could stop their witness. To silence his preaching Luke was hanged on an olive tree, according to tradition. James, brother of Jesus, who once ridiculed Jesus, was beaten, stoned, and had his brains dashed out by a club. Mark was dragged to pieces by people. Peter was crucified upside down. "Martyr" means witness.

A conductor was rehearsing the final practice of a great choir for *The Messiah*. He had reached the point where the soprano soloist took up the refrain, "I know that my Redeemer liveth." The soloist's technique was perfect with faultless breathing, accurate note-placing, flawless enunciation. After the final note all eyes fell on the conductor to catch his approval. Instead he silenced the orchestra. Walking toward the singer he said, "My daughter, do you really know that your Redeemer liveth? Do you?"

"Why, yes," she answered, flushing.

"Then sing it!" cried the conductor. "Tell it to me so that I will know, and so that all who hear you will know the joy and the truth of it!" Then he beckoned the orchestra to play again. This time she sang the truth as she really knew it. All who heard thrilled to the announcement, so convincingly sung, that the conquering Redeemer had risen from the dead.

When this message grips us, how can we keep still?

4

A New Lease on Life

The Lord hath appeared to
Simon.   —Luke 24:34

A psychoanalyst might have had a difficult time with Peter. Exasperating, though colorful, impetuous, blundering, blustering, spouting, trigger-fingered, he blew hot and cold in almost the same breath. Someone termed him as stable as a teen-age girl going steady.

So full of contradiction, he is a combination of courage and cowardice, of faith and unbelief. First to affirm Christ's deity, he immediately followed with "not so, Lord" to his Master's prediction of crucifixion. With sufficient trust he walked on the sea, only to begin to sink through lack of faith. Within seconds of refusing the Lord, "Thou shalt never wash my feet" (John 13:8), he contradicted himself, "not my feet only, but also my hands and my head" (v. 9). He shrank before a maid, but later stood for Christ before a multitude. Weak at first, he was destined to strengthen his brethren. Paradoxically, he was a wavering rock.

Because perfect people make us uncomfortable, we feel affinity with human, prone-to-failure Peter. However, we should not compare ourselves with Peter in the days of his failure. The shortest person finds himself taller than the biggest giant when he measures himself against the giant reclining horizontally on the ground. Likewise, weak Christians feed their spiritual self-satisfaction by comparing themselves with Peter, flat because of his fall. Not Peter down, but Peter restored and up, as he moves boldly through the pages of Acts, may dwarf our spiritual status and provide a more proper model to follow. The major factor in making a new Peter was Christ's appearance to him that first Easter.

Some time during that first Easter Day the risen Lord contacted Simon Peter. Later that evening the disciples behind closed doors buzzed with the news, "The Lord is risen indeed, and hath appeared to Simon" (Luke 24:-34). In his list of those to whom Christ appeared, Paul places Peter first. "He was seen of Cephas, then of the twelve" (1 Cor. 15:5). Though Mary Magdalene was the first person to see the resurrected Saviour, Peter was the first of the apostles.

Of all the disciples Peter needed this visit most. Always first in the list of Jesus' followers, invariably foremost in blurting out questions, also strongest in affirming his undying loyalty to Jesus, Peter had blatantly and shamefully denied his Lord in the hour of his Master's greatest need. His verbal faithlessness ingloriously outshone the inconstancy of all other disciples. Desperately forlorn and wretched, he probably moped about in a daze, half-crazed with bitter remorse over his cowardly denial. But the Lord knew a searing iron was smarting his soul, so he appeared to Peter privately. What relief when Peter sobbed out his repentance to receive the forgiveness of his merciful Master! A new lease on life surged through the restored apostle!

Peter's Need

The evening before his crucifixion the Lord predicted that all his disciples would forsake him. When Peter insisted on his fidelity, even if all others should flee, the Lord prophesied that on that very night before the cock would crow twice Peter would deny him three times. Then Peter boasted, "If I should die with thee, I will not deny thee" (Mark 14:31).

Loud protestation often precedes low performance. The biggest braggadocio in the camp may turn out to be the biggest coward in the conflict. The best swimmer may be in greatest danger of drowning. Overconfidence may lead to carelessness.

Had someone revealed to Peter in advance the horrendous details of his denial, he might have asked, "Am I a dog that I would do that?" As the battle ebbed and flowed over the field at Waterloo, Napoleon—strongest in guns, materiel, officers, and in every way—actually sent three messages to Paris stating he had won the victory. Peter's sad experience led him to write later, "Be clothed with humility" (1 Peter 5:5). Peter would well give assent to Paul's injunction, "Wherefore let him that thinketh he standeth take heed lest he fall" (1 Cor. 10:12). Says the poet, William Cowper:

> Beware of Peter's word,
>   Nor confidently say,
> "I never will deny Thee, Lord!"
>   But, "Grant I never may!"

Spiritual negligence followed Peter's first assertion. A little later in Gethsemane's garden the Lord asked the inner three—Peter, James, and John—to watch and pray. But while their Master agonized midst the gnarled olive trees, they slept. After such a warning about his denial, Peter should have zealously thrown himself in supplication for divine help. Instead, he slumbered physically and spiritually. The Lord chided his boastful follower, "What, could ye not watch with me one hour?" (Matt. 26:40).

Suddenly like giant fireflies in the distance flashed the torches of an approaching mob. Impetuous Peter drew his sword, recklessly swung at the nearest enemy, intending to make two out of him, but instead severed the right ear of Malchus, servant to the high priest. Jesus rebuked Peter, then healed the servant's ear. Peter ran.

Minutes later when the murmur of voices faded and flickering torches disappeared across the brook, Peter realized they were taking away his Master to die. Stumbling back to the path, twigs stinging his face and ripping his robe, he hurried to catch the procession. But he kept his distance, not anxious to get too close after wounding the high priest's servant.

The crowd headed for the house of Annas. At the gate a maid scrutinized those entering. To Peter's surprise he found a friend there, probably John, whose influence succeeded in getting both in. Looking more closely at Peter, she exclaimed, "Art not thou also one of this man's disciples?" Immediately he retorted, "I am not" (John 18:17).

Peter, we stand aghast! Weren't you with the Lord

for three years? Haven't you just taken the Lord's Supper? Don't you remember the day when at his command you cast your net down and you couldn't handle all the fish because there were so many? Has shock obliterated your memory?

Because the night was frosty, the servants lit a fire in the open quadrangle. Peter huddled near the fire. His inner nature pulsated with sympathy for Christ, but he wanted all around to believe him indifferent to the prisoner. The conversation ranged from coarse jokes to latest tidbits from Rome. Suddenly he was jolted to reality from his semidreaming when a maid walked up, poked a lantern under his face, exclaiming, "This man was with him!" Others joined her accusation. Immediately he responded, "I do not know the man." This time he added an oath, calling God in heaven to witness to his statement that he never knew Jesus.

Peter, wait a minute! Remember how you saw him restore sight to blind Bartimaeus! Recall the lame man at the pool of Bethesda! How could you forget the raising of Lazarus?

An hour elapsed. To cover his nervousness, Peter joined the chatter periodically. But his accent gave him away. A man confidently affirmed, "Of a truth this fellow was also with him: for he is a Galilean!" (Luke 22:59). Then Peter emitted a torrent of swearing, as for the third time he denied that he knew Jesus. In the garden he had let loose with his sword; now he lets loose with his tongue, swearing, not like a trooper, but like a Galilean fisherman.

At that moment the soldiers were leading Jesus

away. Peter's strident voice carried through the courtyard, echoing its denials and curses. As the vehement flow of oaths dwindled to silence, the cock crowed the second time. Something struck home to Peter's conscience. He remembered the Lord's prophecy. Just at that moment Jesus turned and looked at Peter. What a look! The Lord had heard every blistering denial, every foul oath. Their eyes met for one moment. Then hot tears flooded Peter's eyes, blurring his vision. He turned and rushed into the cool night air, weeping bitterly.

Peter slept little that night. The next day he wept again and again. He could not forget that look. Guilt burned in his soul—falsehood, evasion, ingratitude, cowardice, profanity—aggravated by his great privilege of three years in the company of Jesus as first among the disciples, after solemn warnings by Jesus, and in the hour of his Master's greatest need. This once eager and devoted apostle cringed like a whipped dog, life crushed from him, nursing shame, almost beside himself with despair. How he needed a new lease on life!

The Meeting with Jesus

Except for the bare mention of the meeting between Jesus and Peter by both Luke and Paul, no record exists of this interview, so sacred and private was its nature.

Yet all those desperate days the Lord's eyes followed Peter, whom he loved despite his failure. Then early that first Easter came the initial word from the Lord, sent to cheer Peter's fallen spirit. An angel at the tomb had given the women the message, "He is risen . . . tell his disciples and Peter" (Mark 16:6-7). This special message of comfort, naming Peter specifically, removed some of his anguish. His Master still cared for him! Mercy was replacing misery. Perhaps after all he could be forgiven for his infamy. As soon as Mary Magdalene brought the word, Peter and John hurried to the sepulcher. John outran Peter, not only because of his youth, but also because Peter's yet-not-fully-dispelled dejection made his legs lumber heavily along.

Later, either that morning or early afternoon, Christ confronted Peter. Wistfully we wonder where. Because Peter had been in John's company, some suggest that on the night of bitter weeping he had been found by John, who took the brokenhearted Peter home with him. In this private interview with the Lord all the shame of the denial Peter blurted out in full confession to receive superabounding remission.

Perhaps Jesus spoke something like this. "Simon, remember how I told you I must die and the third day rise. You were so upset about the cross that you never understood about the rising. Simon, recall how I warned you that you would deny me. But I told you I would pray for you that your faith fail not. It hasn't failed. Simon, I went to the cross for all your sins. Now I'm the living Lord. Your denials are forgiven. Grieve no more!"

Christ had prayed for Peter. He had also given him such a look that Peter went out to weep bitterly. Now he had privately rehabilitated him. But because his denial had been public, the Master arranged a public restoration as well.

Public Affirmation

The account of Peter's public reinstatement comprises an appendage to the Gospel of John. Written to show the deity of Christ, the book reaches its climax in Thomas' confession, "My Lord and my God" (20:28). Then comes this digressive epilogue containing the lovely story of Peter's public restoration. If this incident were omitted, we might puzzle at Peter's leadership in the upper room and his preaching at Pentecost, since our last full view would have portrayed him a blaspheming, Christ-denying failure. After his discrediting experience, the story in the last chapter of John accredits Peter to the reader of the New Testament. Because the veil was drawn tightly over the private meeting of Jesus and Peter, the epilogue explains how in less than two months the Peter of denials became the Peter of Pentecost.

Back in Galilee not long after the resurrection, with the evening breeze wafting along the shore, Peter said, "I go a fishing" (21:3). The same leader was joined by several of the same men in the same occupation, using the same boat on the same lake to suffer the same failure as when a few years back they had toiled all night without a catch. On the shore stood the same Master who, performing the same miracle of an immense catch, showed them again that without him their usual occupation was fruitless. Told to cast the net on the right side, they weren't able to draw the haul which numbered 153 fish. With a flash of recognition Peter plunged toward shore, waiting for no one.

When all the disciples gathered around the fire built

by the Lord and were eating a meal prepared by him, he broached the unfinished business at hand. Peter had publicly denied the Lord. Now he must be publicly restored. Graciously the Lord had dealt with Peter in privacy. But after private reconciliation must be public reinstatement. The scene exhibited several similarities to the night of shame. The denial came after eating the Lord's Supper; now they had just dined. Denials were made around the fire in the courtyard; now they sat around burning coals. Before the denial, reference had been made to a smitten shepherd and scattered sheep; now the command will be, "Feed my sheep." Three denials had been made; now three affirmations must be given.

So the Lord asks, "Simon, lovest thou me?" A certain king gave all his major officers a new name suggested by their qualities. When they displeased him, he reverted to their old name which caused alarm. When he resumed the new name they knew they had regained his favor. Perhaps the Lord's use of Peter's old name, Simon, was designed to remind him of the treachery of his old nature.

Three times Peter answered in effect, "Yea, Lord, thou knowest that I love thee." Before his denial he had boasted of love that exceeded the devotion of others— "Though all men shall be offended because of thee, yet will I never be offended" (Matt. 26:33). Now no protestation of superior love escapes his lips. Rather a humble but sincere, "Thou knowest that I love thee." In fact, Peter, void of all braggadocio, used a milder word to pledge his love than the word for "love" Jesus

employed in his first two questions. The third time the
Lord descended to Peter's more moderate word. Then
the Lord told Peter he would pay for his love with his
life. Tradition says Peter was crucified upside down at
his own request because he deemed himself unworthy
to die like his Master.

Through the pages of Peter's life, many truths have
been etched more clearly. This denial experience has
provided the backdrop for the display of the restoring
mercy of God. Because Peter failed as he did, we know
of God's grace in forgiveness.

An army chaplain heard a knock on his office door.
A man, the picture of misery, entered mumbling, "I've
hauled down the flag, sir!" The soldier standing before
the chaplain was his right-hand assistant who constantly
invited servicemen to the chapel and was a strong influence for good in the barracks. He could always sing a
solo. "I was out with the boys last night and they got
me to drink. They had to carry me back to my quarters.
I'm ashamed of myself. I've hauled down the flag."

Trying to hide his disappointment, the chaplain
countered, "Even if you've hauled down the flag, you
know enough about the mercy of Christ and his power
to haul the flag up again."

"Yes, sir, I've confessed to God. I know he has forgiven me. But how can I ever face the boys again?"

The chaplain stood to his feet. "We're going to kneel
down right here, both of us, and consecrate ourselves
anew to God. Tonight we'll have the regular service
and I want you to sing a solo. It will be hard, but don't
fail to turn up."

That night when his name was announced to sing, everyone gasped. Some smirked, "What an old hypocrite!" The soldier began, "Boys, you know all about me, and the chaplain knows too. I hauled down the flag last night, but by God's grace I've hauled it up again." Then he told how he had confessed his sin to God, and how the wonderful love of Christ welcomed him back. He concluded, "Will you let me sing to you again?" Muffled murmurs gave assent. The soldier sang,

> When I fear my faith will fail,
>   Christ will hold me fast;
> When the tempter would prevail,
>   He can hold me fast.[1]

The next day one of the soldiers asked to speak with the chaplain. "I was one of the men who tempted your soloist to drink the other night. We thought it was a joke. But I tell you, when I heard him sing last night, I called on God to forgive me. From now on I'm going to live for him!"

A Latin hymn alleges that Peter never heard a cock crow without falling to his knees to weep. One tradition says that he was accustomed to wake daily at cockcrow to spend an hour in prayer, the fatal hour in which he had failed his Lord. Though without basis in fact, these traditions do suggest that Peter's life was stronger because of his fall.

[1] "He Hauled Down the Flag," from *The Challenge*, Auckland, New Zealand.

See him on the day of Pentecost facing thousands of people, "Him . . . ye have taken, and by wicked hands have crucified and slain: whom God hath raised up" (Acts 2:23-24).

Hear him after the healing of the lame man at the gate Beautiful, "Ye . . . killed the Prince of life, whom God hath raised from the dead; whereof we are witnesses" (Acts 3:14-15).

Listen as he addresses the Sanhedrin, the same council which engineered his Master's death, giving the reason for the lame man's healing, "Be it known unto you all . . . that by the name of Jesus Christ of Nazareth, whom ye crucified, whom God raised from the dead, even by him doth this man stand here before you whole. . . . Neither is there salvation in any other: for there is none other name under heaven given among men, whereby we must be saved" (Acts 4:10-12).

What made Peter a new man? Meeting Christ in that private rendezvous that first Easter gave Peter a new lease on life. No wonder Peter could write, "Blessed be the God and Father of our Lord Jesus Christ, which according to his abundant mercy hath begotten us again unto a lively hope by the resurrection of Jesus Christ from the dead" (1 Peter 1:3).

5

The Burning Heart

*Did not our heart burn within
us?*   —Luke 24:32

A missionary and a statesman, Robert E. Speer, once talked with a young Chinese Christian who was preaching the gospel in the interior of China. He was a college graduate who had come a thousand miles from his home to bring the good tidings to his fellow countrymen.

After Dr. Speer had questioned him at length concerning the spiritual status of national Christians, the young man said, "Mr. Speer, you have asked me many questions. Some have been difficult. Now I would like to ask you one question. You know what the Christians in your country are like. Are they all men and women of burning hearts?"

Dr. Speer pertinently commented, "What would you have answered him?"

Understandably, for many who are not Christians life has lost its meaning. One man who took his life left this note, "I am not really needed. Nobody cares for me. I am just a peanut at Yankee stadium." These definitions

of life appeared in a college newspaper: "Life is a bad
joke which isn't even funny"; "Life is a disease for
which the only cure is death"; "Life is a jail sentence
which we get for the crime of being born."

However, many who are Christians walk the path of
life sad, defeated, and lonely—even though in the company of another, like the two disciples on the Emmaus
road that first Easter. Early that afternoon they left
Jerusalem for what turned out to be the strangest walk
of their lives. Their hearts were cold and ashen, because
a few days before the one on whom they had pinned
their messianic hope had been cruelly crucified. That
morning astonishing news that Jesus' tomb was empty
had reached them. But in unbelief they headed home to
Emmaus, seven miles away, a walk of approximately
two hours. On the way a guest joined them whose
conversation warmed their chilly hearts and whose revelation in their home at the end of the trip changed night
to day. Of all the stories of Christ's resurrection appearances, none so fascinates as this episode with its
dramatic vividness, definiteness of detail, and delightful
simplicity.

Who were these disciples? Only one is named, Cleopas, a person hard to identify. Tradition makes him an
uncle of Jesus, supposedly because either he is brother
to Joseph or his wife is sister to Mary. Many think his
companion is his wife. One wise scholar suggested, "The
learned cannot come to any agreement who the other
was and I will give you this good counsel. Let each of
you take his place."

Their thoughts were retrospective, not prospective,

because there seemed to be no future. Miserable, despairing, disappointed, they slouched along. The road to Emmaus was a sad walk. But the return trip was to be a joyous one because it was prompted by a burning heart. How did they acquire this flaming spirit?

Kindled by the Scriptures

Engaged in earnest conversation on recent happenings, they failed to notice the sudden approach of a stranger they should have recognized. But their last gaze at him had rested on a scarred and broken form. He asked what they were talking about and why they were sad. What tender humor! Imagine the Saviour, whom they thought dead and buried in Joseph's sepulcher, asking the topic of their conversation, when all the time he was that object of their discussion!

They expressed amazement that anyone in the Jerusalem area would be ignorant of the leading news of the last few days. The events had been so public that any stranger, even a one-night lodger in the city, could not have missed them. "What things?" the Lord asked, continuing to play with them in pretended ignorance.

As the three walked slowly, the two gave an excited, jumbled report in which hope and despair struck alternate chords. The one whom they had expected would redeem Israel had been crucified. Though women of their group had reported the tomb empty and Jesus alive, obstinate unbelief throttled hope. Their remarks, staccatoed out with the impulsive language of intense feeling, evidenced a love for their Master which even the grave could not extinguish.

Then the Lord chided them. "O fools, and slow of heart to believe all that the prophets have spoken: Ought not Christ to have suffered these things, and to enter into his glory?" (Luke 24:25-26). He didn't rebuke them for disbelieving the reports about the resurrection but for negligence in accepting the Scriptures.

Then was preached the first postresurrection sermon. The preacher was the Lord Jesus; the congregation, two Jewish peasants; the time, the first Easter afternoon; the place, a country road running between Jerusalem and Emmaus; the theme, that Jesus Christ is found throughout the Old Testament. Beginning with the Pentateuch and proceeding to the Prophets, Jesus taught them how the Old Testament predicted his sufferings and victory over death.

What a sermon that must have been! The greatest course in Old Testament was given by our Lord in this and similar discourses during his forty-day sojourn on earth before his ascension. Not only did he appear several times to his disciples to prove incontrovertibly his resurrection, but he also opened their understanding of the Scriptures. Without doubt, many of the apostles' references to Old Testament verses fulfilled by Christ's ministry were pointed out firsthand by our Lord in these sessions. Most likely he showed the Emmaus disciples how the Passover lamb, the scapegoat on the Day of Atonement, and the brass serpent all portrayed the cross which they had just witnessed. He pointed out in the Prophets specific references to his death and resurrection. Christ at once became both magnificent theme and marvelous expositor of the Scriptures. Had he not said,

"Search the scriptures; . . . they are they which testify of me" (John 5:39)?

How tragic that many people rarely read their Bibles. A judge said to a woman, "If you can say the Lord's Prayer, you can go free." She replied, "Now I lay me down to sleep; I pray the Lord my soul to keep." He responded, "You may go free!"

A preacher asked a little girl if she attended Sunday school regularly. When she replied yes, he asked, "Do you know what's in your Bible?" "Sure," she replied, "Sister's boy friend's picture's in it, and Ma's recipe for vanishing cream, and a lock of my hair when I was a baby, and oh, yes, a ticket for Pa's watch is in it."

A Bible in every room in the house will do no good unless it is rightly used to find therein the living Christ.

"Did not our heart burn within us, while he talked with us by the way, and while he opened to us the scriptures?" (Luke 24:32). For such an experience, we must learn to find the Lord Jesus in his Word.

John Wesley's spiritual birthday took place during the evening of May 24, 1738. He was attending a meeting in Aldersgate Street, London. Here the leader read Luther's preface to the book of Romans. Says Wesley, "About a quarter before nine, while he was describing the change which God works in the heart through faith in Christ, I felt my heart strangely warmed; I felt I did trust Christ, Christ alone, for salvation: and an assurance was given me, that he had taken away *my* sins, even *mine*, and saved *me* from the law of sin and death. I began to pray with all my might for those who had in a more especial manner despitefully used me and persecuted me. I then testified openly to all there what I now first felt in my heart."[1] That heart warmed by the Word of God went out to shake England for God.

Growth in the Christian life does not happen suddenly, magically, or automatically, but through the Word. "Now ye are clean through the word which I have spoken unto you" (John 15:3). "Sanctify them through thy truth: thy word is truth" (17:17). "That he might sanctify and cleanse it [the church] with the washing of water by the word" (Eph. 5:26). "As newborn babes, desire the sincere milk of the word, that ye may grow thereby" (1 Peter 2:2). Feeding on Christ warms the heart, strengthens the soul, and gives zest and purpose to life. Even the Lord Jesus saturated himself in the Word, for when Satan tempted him, he resisted through the Word, three times answering, "It is written," and in each case quoting from Deuteronomy.

People sometimes ask, "What can we do on Sunday after church?" Too often Christians make a holiday out of the Lord's Day. Could not we learn from the Emmaus disciples who meditated on the Word some of those hours between noon and evening? What better way could we spend time on Sunday afternoon than feeding on Christ through the Bible?

Warmed by Christ's Fellowship

The trio neared Emmaus. As they turned into their home, the stranger took a step away from them, as if to go on. The Lord never forced himself on people. They

[1]Robert Southey, *The Life of Wesley* (London: Longman, Brown, Green, Longmans, and Roberts, 1858), I, 101.

constrained him to enter. "Abide with us: for it is toward evening, and the day is far spent" (Luke 24:29).

Henry F. Lyte, English clergyman, informed by his
doctor of a serious illness and of need for a change of
climate, preached his farewell sermon on a September
Sunday morning over a century ago near the Devon-
shire coast of England. Later that afternoon as the
shadows began to lengthen, he took a walk in the woods,
then wrote the words of the well-known hymn, "Abide
with Me," based on the invitation of the Emmaus disciples, "Abide with us." He sensed a deep need for
the presence and power of Christ as he neared the end
of his journey.

Christ was so easily invited. It probably took a few
minutes to throw some food together, particularly since
they had spent the holiday season at Jerusalem and now
needed to light a fire. With the meal finally ready they
sat down at the table. Strangely the guest, reversing his
role, became the host. He took bread, blessed, broke,
and gave to them—a task normally performed by the
entertainer. When Christ is welcomed into any life he
takes over to preside at the banquet table of grace.

Suddenly, as the Lord broke bread, they recognized
him! They had seen him break bread before—at the feeding of the five thousand, of the four thousand, in the
upper room. So frequently the risen Lord was recognized, not by his appearance as by some familiar ges-
ture. They ejaculated, looking at each other in surprise.
But before they could embrace him, he vanished, his
body no longer subject to earthly order. Then it was
they remarked how their hearts burned within as he

talked with them by the way. Fellowship with Christ warms the heart. Those who walk the discouraged Emmaus road with hopes dashed and prospects dim may invite into their lives the only one who can bring meaning and exhilaration.

Bishop Handley Moule wrote a hymn which appears in the *Keswick Hymnal* and is often sung in England:

Come in, O come! the door stands open now;
I knew Thy voice; Lord Jesus, it was Thou;
The sun has set long since; the storms begin;
'Tis time for Thee, My Savior, O come in!

Alas, ill-ordered shows the dreary room;
The household-stuff lies heaped amidst the gloom,
The table empty stands, the couch undressed;
Ah, what a welcome for th' Eternal guest!

Yet welcome, and tonight; this doleful scene
Is e'en itself my cause to hale Thee in;
This dark confusion e'en at once demands
Thine own bright presence, Lord, and ord'ring hands.

I seek no more to alter things, or mend,
Before the coming of so great a Friend;
All were at best unseemly; and 'twere ill
Beyond all else to keep Thee waiting still.

Come, not to find, but make this troubled heart
A dwelling worthy of Thee as Thou art;
To chase the gloom, the terror, and the sin:
Come, all Thyself, yea come, Lord Jesus, in!

Glowed into Action

Consternation reigned in that little home. Then, their hearts, kindled by the Word, warmed by his fellowship, now ignited into action. Their "glowing" led to "going."

Joy flooded their hearts. The one on whom their hopes had rested was not dead. He was alive! They felt compelled to communicate that knowledge to others. How could they leave loved ones in ignorance when they had experienced the fervor of his presence?

Though darkness was soon to set in, they decided to return to Jerusalem immediately. Traveling in the dark took courage. Besides, they were extremely tired. For these very reasons they had invited the stranger into their home. But somehow their weariness had fled. Their feet which dragged on the journey to Emmaus now seemed to fly on the return trip. The seven miles which coming seemed like seventeen now floated by like one-quarter the distance. Every step was filled with memory. Passing a certain rock, Cleopas would say, "Remember, it was here he told us he was the rock!" At another point, "Recall here he said he was the Lamb of God!" At still another spot, "Here he told he was the scape-goat!"

With throbbing hearts and soaring spirits they hurried into Jerusalem, down narrow streets, then knocked at a closed door. Cautiously the door opened a little. After joyful greetings they learned that the Lord had appeared to Peter. Then the Emmaus couple reported their story, which the disciples disbelieved till Jesus came and stood in their midst to demonstrate its truth.

The home in Emmaus was never the same. How often husbands and wives testify, "Once we cared not for the Bible, the church, or Christ. Now life is different. We can't wait for Sunday to come to meet the Lord in his house to worship and study!" Touched by the risen

Christ their hearts now glow with the glory of the gospel.

On fire for the Lord the early church so turned the world upside down that in three centuries one tenth of the Roman Empire was Christian. Early in the fourth century Christianity was declared the state religion. The same burning heart propelled Livingstone out to Africa, keeping him there under most difficult circumstances, away from his wife and children. A Hollywood director once showed a seminary professor around a movie studio which was engaged in the production of the picture *With Stanley in Africa*. He remarked, "I have a problem. To reproduce jungle scenes and animal life is easy. But I am finding it difficult to portray the power that sent Livingstone to Africa and kept him there midst almost insuperable odds till death." The seminary professor could have answered, "Livingstone's burning heart!"

The consumed heart sends out missionaries today, like the five young men martyred by the Auca Indians. The glowing spirit sent back one of the widows to work among the people who took her husband's life, enabling her to *love* and *win* all the assassins to Christ.

In the middle of the night a church caught on fire. The reflection of the conflagration revealed an atheist, running with the crowd toward the disaster. Someone asked, "Why is it that we could never get you to go to church, but now you are headed that way?" The atheist retorted, "I would go any day in the week to see a church on fire!" We need churches and Christians aglow for God!

At a ministers' conference a pastor told how some years before a baby had been born into their family. "This little bundle from heaven, so far as we could tell, was a perfect baby and the brightness of our home for three years. Then one day he took sick. The doctors were baffled. Specialists could not discover the trouble. One day we gathered around the tiny crib. Our family doctor was there. The little fellow's pulse grew fainter and fainter until the doctor pronounced him dead. I looked at my wife. Then I asked for hot blankets. I tore open my shirt. I took that little limp form and clasped it to my breast. My wife wrapped the warm blankets around me. For nine hours I held that form over my heart." Then he turned to the ministers, "My boy today is twenty-two years of age. He is a senior in college and doing a wonderful work for Christ!"

We need hearts rekindled with fire from above, which in turn will bring warmth and zest to the multitudes whose hearts are cold and ashen.

6

The Wounds of Christ

Behold my hands and my feet.
—Luke 24:39

A standard course in first aid classifies four types of wounds which can be remembered by the word *p-a-i-l.* "P" stands for puncture, "A" for abrasion, "I" for incision, and "L" for laceration.

Remarkably, the Lord Jesus Christ suffered all four types. His hands and feet were punctured by nails. His brow was scraped abrasively. His side was pierced incisively. His back was torn and lacerated. Even more noteworthy, in heaven today he still bears the marks of those wounds. Matthew Bridges, the hymn writer, said,

> Crown Him the Lord of love!
> Behold His hands and side,—
> Rich wounds, yet visible above,
> In beauty glorified:
> No angel in the sky
> Can fully bear that sight,
> But downward bends his wondering eye
> At mysteries so bright.

Marks of Recognition

Victims of tragedies are often identified by scars. After a fierce battle, the queen of an ancient empire left her palace to hunt among the victims on the field for her warrior-husband. Suddenly the torch dropped from her hand, as gazing on a prostrate form, she cried, "I have found him! I know him by his scars!" In Homer's *Odyssey* the old nurse of Ulysses found the final proof of her master's identity when she discovered the remembered scar on his leg.

Early that first Easter rumors of Christ's resurrection began to circulate among the disciples, causing consternation. At even, some of them assembled behind closed doors for fear of the Jews. Jesus came and stood in the midst of them. Thinking him a ghost, they were terror-stricken. But he reassured them by showing them his hands, feet, and side (cf. Luke 24:39; John 20:20). He invited them to handle him and see.

How often the disciples had seen those hands touch blind eyes, break bread, bless little children, dispel leprosy, and even raise the dead. Now those hands bore nailprints. The wounds were marks of recognition. How often they had seen those sandaled feet pace the dusty paths of Palestine. Now these same feet were pierced. The wounds were marks of recognition. He was the very same Jesus.

The disciples excitedly reported the amazing news to Thomas, who was not present that first Sunday night. Skeptically he reacted, "Except I shall see in his hands the print of the nails, and put my finger into the print of the nails, and thrust my hand into his side, I will not

believe" (John 20:25). The next Sunday Thomas was
present when our Lord appeared. Turning to Thomas,
the Lord invited him to reach his finger into his palm
and thrust his hand into his side. But Thomas immediately recognized those hands and side. Argument turned
to adoration as he exclaimed, "My Lord and my God"
(v. 28).

When Christ returns to earth in glory, he may be
recognized by his wounds. "Behold, he cometh with
clouds; and every eye shall see him, and they also which
pierced him: and all kindreds of the earth shall wail
because of him" (Rev. 1:7).

How will the saints recognize Christ in heaven? Not
by his pictures, for no reliable likeness of him exists.
Most paintings stem from medieval conceptions, usually
too effeminate. A scene in heaven in John's apocalyptic
vision focuses on the exalted Saviour. "Lo, in the midst
of the throne . . . stood a Lamb as it had been slain"
(Rev. 5:6). The expression "as it had been slain" im-
plies the marks of the slaying are still evident. The
clause could rightly read, "stood a Lamb with the marks
of its death." The Lamb is none other than the Lord
Jesus Christ, for a few sentences later the Lamb is re-
ferred to as having "redeemed us to God by thy blood
out of every kindred" (v. 9). Undoubtedly one of the
ways we shall know the Lord in glory will be by his
marks. Says the hymn writer, Fanny J. Crosby,

> I shall know Him, I shall know Him,
>   And redeemed by His side I shall stand,
> I shall know Him, I shall know Him
>   By the print of the nails in His hand.

Marks of Suffering

Intense, indeed, were the sufferings of the victim of crucifixion. Often the victim was nailed to the cross before it was lifted up. Held horizontally on the cross on the ground while soldiers readied to pound a spike through his hand, the victim usually swore, squirmed, spat, screamed, and struggled. Soon blood would spurt as one hand was transfixed. Then the other hand. Then with legs pushed up, the knees out, so that the soles of the feet were flat against the vertical beam, nails were banged through the feet. All this time the victim gave vent to his pain by hurling the most blasphemous oaths at his executors. To the amazement of the soldiers, Jesus offered no resistance. He went as a lamb to the slaughter. Instead of reviling, he prayed, "Father, forgive them; for they know not what they do" (Luke 23:34).

Lifted up, the cross was then dropped into a hole in the ground with a jar that would jolt every bone in the body. Then would follow hours of agony. Historians tell us that often severe local inflammation, coupled with minor bleeding, produced fever which was aggravated by the strained and crushing weight of the body, the insufferable thirst, the implacable swarms of torturing insects, and the relentless rays of the sun which beat down in the case of Jesus for three hours prior to noon before mercifully hiding its face. Torn tendons caused excruciating pain, especially in the hands— the seat of keen sensibility. Arteries of head and stomach were surcharged with blood, resulting in a throbbing, pounding headache. Sometimes convulsions would tear at the wounds, till with bodily forces exhausted, the victim would sink into unconsciousness. The victim of crucifixion literally died a thousand deaths.

Deeper than his physical sufferings were Christ's soul agonies. For his soul was made an offering for sin. He whose very nature of holiness was repulsed by iniquity was somehow made iniquity. He who knew no sin was made sin for us, so that realizing the Father's rejection he cried out, "My God, my God, why hast thou forsaken me?" (Matt. 27:46; Mark 15:34).

This suffering was for us. "He was wounded for our transgressions, he was bruised for our iniquities: the chastisement of our peace was upon him; and with his stripes we are healed" (Isa. 53:5). Those who try to gain heaven by doing the best they can, by keeping the Golden Rule, by obeying the Ten Commandments, or by treating their neighbors as themselves, really say, "See my hands. They are sufficient to earn my salvation. Christ, I don't need your nail-pierced hands!" Such an attitude insults Christ's death. As Paul put it, "If righteousness come by the law [doing good works], then Christ is dead in vain" (Gal. 2:21). But because we could not possibly atone for our sins, no matter how moral we might be, Christ left heaven to bear the penalty on the cross that we might not perish but have everlasting life.

The scars of Christ will not be blemishes but marks of beauty. A little fellow asked his mother, "Why are your hands ugly and scarred? They're not pretty like the hands of other mothers." Quiet for a moment, she replied, "Let me tell you a story. One day when you were a very little lad you were playing in the backyard, when some boys in the neighborhood built a fire in our alley. When the boys left, you toddled up to the fire and fell. I heard your screams, rushed out, beat out the flames with my hands. You were scarcely burned. But my hands were burned, and scarred terribly. That's why they're ugly!" The little fellow thought a moment, then blurted out, "Mother, your hands aren't ugly. They're beautiful!" Says the poet,

> They nailed those beautiful, blessed hands
>   To the cruel, bitter cross,
> And there, in agony untold,
>   He bore our shame and loss.
> Beautiful hands of Jesus!
>   I hope some day to see
> Those wonderful, loving, nail-scarred hands
>   That were pierced on Calvary.[1]

In heaven the perpetual reminder of our Saviour's sufferings will remove the need for observing the Lord's Supper. The main reason for observing the Lord's Supper is our short memories; they need periodic jogging on the loving sacrifice of Christ. The symbols of broken bread and red juice vividly recall his crucified body and shed blood. But in glory graphic evidence displayed by the marks on his body will ever stir our devotion.

Marks of Victory

Scars indicate a battle fought, and often a victory won. Christ entered the arena of spiritual conflict and emerged victor over Satan, sin, and death. Scathed in the struggle,

[1] From *The Gospel Witness*, East Toronto, Ontario, Canada. Reprinted by permission.

he bears wounds which signify victory. The poet has put it,

> Thy wounds, thy wounds, Lord Jesus,
>   Those deep, deep wounds will tell
> The sacrifice that frees us
>   From self, and death, and hell!
> These link Thee once for ever
>   With all who own Thy grace:
> No hand these bonds can sever,
>   No hand these scars efface.[2]

If Satan, the accuser of the brethren, should appear before the Father in heaven to denounce—"Look at that man down there on earth. Look at his many sins. How can you call him your child?"—the Lord Jesus would merely need to lift his hands. The Father, seeing the marks, would remember Calvary where his Son shed his blood for the remission of sins. Satan would slink away in defeat. The wound marks are the badge of a lawyer who never loses a case.

One day as Napoleon looked over the map of Europe with his lieutenants, pointing to the various nations, he said, "We can conquer these easily." Then he put his finger on the British Isles, exclaiming, "But for this red spot we could conquer the whole world!" But for the red spot of Calvary, evidence of which Christ still carries in his hands, feet, and side, Satan might have conquered. Charles Wesley wrote,

> Arise, my soul, arise!
>   Shake off thy guilty fears;

[2] Quoted by Tom Olson in *Now*, January 26, 1940.

The bleeding Sacrifice
  In my behalf appears.
Before the throne my Surety stands;
My name is written on His hands.

. . . .

Five bleeding wounds He bears,
  Received on Calvary;
They pour effectual prayers,
  They strongly plead for me.
"Forgive him, O forgive!" they cry,
"Nor let that ransomed sinner die!"

. . . .

My God is reconciled;
  His pardoning voice I hear:
He owns me for His child;
  I can no longer fear:
With confidence I now draw nigh,
And "Father, Abba, Father!" cry.

A lady seriously ill in the hospital was visited by a clergyman. At the end of the visit he suggested that she might like to confess her sins to him. Unable to see well, she asked him to put his hand in hers. She felt one side, then turned the hand over to feel the other. Gently pushing the hand away, she quietly said, "The hand that forgives my sin must have nailprints in it."

The hands of Christ seem very frail
For they were broken by a nail;
But only they reach heaven at last,
Whom those frail, broken hands hold fast!

JOHN R. MORELAND

To see in the wounds of Christ evidence of sufferings endured as the atonement for our personal sins will mean that these marks guarantee our victory over sin, self, and death. Some day these scars will prove marks of recognition of our Saviour whom, as yet not seeing, we love. In the meantime the nailprints are proof of his right to control our lives.

Marks of Ownership

The wounds of Christ suggest that we have been purchased by the blood of Christ, that we no longer belong to ourselves but are the slaves of Jesus Christ. Paul exclaims, "What? know ye not that your body is the temple of the Holy Ghost which is in you . . . ? For ye are bought with a price: therefore glorify God in your body" (1 Cor. 6:19-20). Peter likewise teaches, "Forasmuch as ye know that ye were not redeemed with corruptible things, as silver and gold . . . but with the precious blood of Christ" (1 Peter 1:18-19).

No longer can those who name the name of Christ say what they wish, look at what they want, do what they desire, or walk where they will. Owned by Christ, our tongues, eyes, hands, and feet—our entire bodies and intellects—belong to him. His wounds are reminders of his ownership.

Three men were playing cards for stakes on a commuter's train. Needing a fourth player, they asked a fellow sitting nearby if he would join them. Politely he declined. After trying several others without success, they again approached the same fellow. When again he graciously refused, they asked why he wouldn't play. He replied, "I have no hands."

"What are those things dangling by your side?"

"Those are hands," he admitted. "But," he added, "not my hands. Two years ago I gave myself to Christ. He owns me now. These hands belong to him. And he doesn't wish them to gamble."

A small orphaned boy lived with his grandmother. One night the house caught on fire. The grandmother, trying to rescue the little lad asleep upstairs, perished in the flames. A crowd gathered round the burning house. The boy's cries for help were heard above the crackling of the blaze. No one seemed to know what to do, for the front of the house was a mass of flames. Suddenly a stranger rushed from the crowd and circled to the back where he spotted an iron pipe that reached to the second floor. Hand over hand he climbed the hot pipe, reached an upstairs window, disappeared for a minute, then reappeared with the boy in his arms. Mid the cheers of the crowd, he climbed down the hot pipe as the boy hung round his neck.

Weeks later a public meeting was held in the town hall to determine in whose custody the boy would be placed. Each person wanting the boy was permitted to speak briefly. The first man spoke, "I have a big farm. Every boy needs the out-of-doors." The second man propounded the advantages he could give the lad. "I'm a teacher. I have a large library. He would get a good education." Others spoke. Finally the richest man in the community said, "I'm wealthy. I could give the boy everything mentioned tonight: farm, books, education, and plenty besides, including money and travel. I would like to have him live in our home."

The chairman asked, "Anyone else like to say a

word?" From the back seat rose a stranger who had slipped unnoticed into the hall. As he walked toward the front, deep suffering showed on his face. Reaching the front of the room, he stood directly in front of the little boy whose custody was being decided. Slowly the stranger removed his hands from his pockets. A gasp went up from the crowd. The little boy whose eyes had been focused on the floor till now looked up. The man's hands were scarred terribly. Suddenly the lad emitted a cry of recognition. Here was the man who had saved his life. His hands were scarred from climbing up and down the hot pipe. With a leap he threw himself around the stranger's neck and held on for life.

The farmer rose and left. The teacher, too. Then the rich man. Everyone departed, leaving the boy and his rescuer who had won him without a word. Those marred hands spoke more effectively than words.

Today many interests vie for our devotion. Young and old alike are challenged by the call of money, education, fame, pleasure, and a host of other voices. But let us never forget that down the corridors of the centuries walks one who, by merely raising his hands, reminds us of his claim upon us. Those hands are nail-pierced. They speak more eloquently than ten thousand sermons. They say,

> I gave my life for thee,
>   My precious blood I shed,
> That thou might'st ransomed be,
>   And quickened from the dead;
> I gave, I gave My life for thee,
> What has thou giv'n for Me?

7

What Thomas Missed

But Thomas . . . was not with them. —*John 20:24*

An elderly man could be seen walking to church every Sunday morning. Neighbors knew he was deaf and could not hear a word of the sermon, the music of the choir, or the hymns sung by the congregation. A scoffer asked, "Why do you spend your Sundays in church when you can't hear a word?" He replied, "I want my neighbors to know which side I'm on!"

Though schools, industry, and offices have their problems of absenteeism, churches suffer most. On a typical Sunday a church with six hundred members will have three hundred or less present. Perhaps churches receive members too laxly, failing to test their depth of commitment. One church in Pennsylvania boasted a large membership. A new pastor discovered that many members never darkened the door of the church. One couple said, "We are not Christians." Asked how their names appeared on the roll, they explained, "A former pastor thought it would be lovely to have fifty new members join one Easter. By the Saturday before, forty-eight had been rounded up. A church official begged us to let our names be proposed for membership so that the goal could be reached next morning. We told him we were not Christians, but he replied that it didn't matter as long as fifty joined!"

Why Was Thomas Absent?

The person who stays away from church, knowingly or unwittingly, votes against church. On the first Easter evening ten of the twelve were gathered in the upper room, plus other followers. Who were the absentees? Thomas and Judas. Judas was not present, for he had taken his own life. Thomas' nonpresence was inexcusable. Christ had chosen the twelve that they might be with him. Thomas was one of the twelve. Others might be excused but not the twelve. Those who occupy positions of leadership in the church carry a special responsibility. Deacons, trustees, elders, teachers, youth advisers, and committee members should not absent themselves from the Lord's house. Whoever else may, leaders ought to be present, setting an example for the flock. But one of the Master's chosen "was not with them" when Christ appeared.

Thomas was not absent because of any lack of love for his Lord. When the other disciples had hesitated to return to Judea because Jesus' life was in jeopardy there, it was Thomas who said, "Let us also go, that we may die with him" (John 11:16). Nor was it lack of interest in spiritual matters. When Jesus had talked about going away, it was Thomas who asked, "We know not

whither thou goest; and how can we know the way?"
His question evoked the Saviour's majestic affirmation,
"I am the way, the truth, and the life" (John 14:5-6).

Why was he missing? The following conjectures,
though not true for Thomas, explain the absence of
many modern Thomases.

His excuse might have been, "I've been hard at
work all day. I'm tired. If I walk half a mile to
the upper room I shall get no good out of the service,
for I'm too sleepy."

Someone wrote a true confession entitled, "Lord, I
Lied!"

Almighty God, as I sit here tonight, surrounded by news-
papers and half watching television, it has just come to me
that I have lied to thee and to myself. I said I was too tired
to go to church tonight. That was not true. I would have
gone to a baseball game, P.T.A. or any other place I had
wanted to go. Being too tired seemed to cover up my in-
difference. God, have mercy on me; I have lied to thee and
to myself. I am not too tired. I am indifferent. Warm my
cold heart, O God, for that is the real reason why I stayed
home. Amen.

Perhaps Thomas had planned to go had the evening
been pleasant. But rain threatened. The streets were
still muddy from a previous shower. His sandals needed
repair. The upper room was quite a walk. Yet rain
and mud do not keep people home from other affairs.

> What matters pelting rain or snow
> If I have tickets for the show?
> But let one drop of rain besmirch
> And it's too wet to go to church.

Maybe Thomas reasoned, "That service will last over an hour. I just can't spare that long. Besides, I can't bear the hot, unventilated room. I'll likely get a headache. Or when I come out into the evening air I might catch cold."

Yet people spend two or three hours at parties or places of amusement where time passes so quickly, despite overcrowded, stuffy rooms.

Remorseful over his own defection, he may have hesitated at going to a worship service. Men whose business dealings have bordered on the shady side do not relish going to the place where people do business with God.

Though people have always given these excuses for absence from church, the real reason Thomas missed that meeting was because he did not expect Jesus to be there. He didn't believe Christ had risen from the dead. He told the others, in effect, "You go and mourn together if you like, but he won't be present."

The Christian mayor of a large Canadian city told his secretary right after his election, "No appointments are to be made for me under any circumstances on Wednesday night." When the secretary looked at him questioningly, the mayor explained, "I have an appointment with my Lord every Wednesday night and I never fail to go meet him. I will meet no one else." While mayor of that city, he maintained his practice of regular attendance at midweek prayer meeting.

The Lord took account of all present and missed someone. Noting Thomas' absence, he inspired John to record it in his Gospel for all posterity to read. The Lord misses us when we miss church. When we miss going to the Lord's house to worship, we deprive ourselves of numerous benefits. Thomas missed several.

The Blessings Thomas Missed

The presence of Christ.—When the rumors of the empty tomb began to circulate, the disciples came together through common attraction to the victim of Calvary. Into their convocation, through closed doors, came Jesus himself and stood in their midst. But Thomas missed him.

The phone rang in the office of a Washington church. "Will the President be in church Sunday morning?" a voice asked. The minister replied, "That I cannot promise. But I do know the Lord will be present, and that should be sufficient incentive for a reasonably large attendance."

When the British queen toured Canada a few years ago, crowds jammed a little church in Niagara Falls one Sunday morning, spilling out on the lawn around the edifice. The people knew that Her Majesty would be there. Our King of kings has promised to be in every service, even where two or three gather in his name. Failure to attend church means foregoing the fellowship of Christ who promised to be where groups gather in his name.

In that upper room the Lord opened the understanding of those present, enabling them to comprehend the Scriptures. As he had done with the Emmaus disciples a few hours previous, he showed how the law of Moses, the Prophets, and the poetical books predicted his sufferings and resurrection. Doubtless their hearts burned within as he illumined their minds. But Thomas missed this insurpassable course in Old Testament interpretation.

The Word of God has been ordained as the instrument of our sanctification. Jesus said, "Sanctify them through thy truth: thy word is truth" (John 17:17). Paul wrote, "Christ also loved the church, and gave himself for it; that he might sanctify and cleanse it with the washing of water by the word" (Eph. 5:25-26). Just as the Lord resisted satanic allurements by quoting the Scriptures, so the Word, learned through church attendance, can help us conquer temptation.

A teen-ager was making an ocean voyage alone. Two unscrupulous men agreed that one of them would persuade him to take a drink of liquor. Drawing near the lad, and in a very pleasant voice, he invited him to drink a glass of wine with him.

"I thank you, sir," replied the boy, "but I never drink intoxicating liquor."

"Never mind, my lad; it will not hurt you. Come and have a drink with me."

" 'Wine is a mocker, strong drink is raging: and whosoever is deceived thereby is not wise,' " said the boy.

"You need not be deceived by it. I would not have you drink much. A little will do you no harm."

" 'At the last it biteth like a serpent, and stingeth like an adder,' " said the boy, "and I certainly think it is wise not to play with an adder."

"My fine young fellow," said the crafty man, "it will give me great pleasure if you will only come and drink just one glass of the best wine with me."

"My Bible says, 'If sinners entice thee, consent thou not,'" was the lad's reply.

Rather stunned, the tempter returned to his friend who asked, "Well, did you succeed?"

"Not at all," grumbled the man. "That youngster is so full of the Bible I can't do a thing with him!"

One mother told her boy, "I always attend both Sunday morning and evening services. Every time I go I learn something new. When you stay away, you miss some truth."

To allay the disciples' fright at seeing what they supposed was a ghost, the Lord showed them his hands, feet, and side. He invited them to handle him to make sure it was he. The nailprints made such an impression that in reporting the appearance of Christ to Thomas they stressed the wounds. This emphasis drew from him his reply of skepticism and demand for a pragmatic test, "Except I shall see in his hands the print of the nails . . . I will not believe" (John 20:25).

At church we come to a deeper appreciation of the sufferings of the Saviour for our sins and of his resurrection for our justification. In God's house we learn that Jesus paid the penalty on the cross, and that God placed his stamp of approval on Calvary's sacrifice by raising Jesus from the dead.

General Gordon, British hero of Khartoum, once saw a young man in danger of being cut to pieces by a fanatical mob. Riding into the midst of the milling mass, Gordon rescued the young man, but in doing so received a deep cut on his face. He had to undergo serious and painful surgery. A few years later the same young man, now a lawyer, became the opponent of General Gordon in a political quarrel. But one evening, going to hear Gordon speak, he saw in the glare of the floodlights the scar on his face. He left the meeting muttering, " I had forgotten the scar. I had forgotten the scar."

Not only the observance of the Lord's Supper but every attendance at church should remind us of Christ's scars, which speak of his sacrificial love and demand our full devotion.

The fellowship of believers.—Though the other ten still had rough spots which needed polishing, association with Christ for three years had molded them into a privileged, trained, and godly group. By his absence, Thomas missed out on the fellowship of the saints.

Admittedly, no church is composed of perfect people. But believers for the most part are God's choicest gems. God established his church as a community where his people would derive strength and growth from mutual worship and interests.

One Monday morning a keen but cynical youth asked his neighbor, an elderly lady who never missed church, what the minister spoke on Sunday morning. "Eh, lad, I can't remember," admitted the lady.

"Well, what was his text?"

"I remember it was a very good sermon but I can't recall what it was about."

"Well, can you tell me what the sermon was about at the evening service?" queried the young man.

"Well, no, I can't say that I can. It seems to have slipped my mind."

The youth smiled. "That's queer. What's the use of

going to church if you can't remember a single word the preacher said?"

The old lady looked at him severely. "Lad," she asked, her voice quivering, "will you do me a favor? Will you take this old clothes basket to the well and bring it back full of water?"

"Come, come," said the young man. "I'm not quite as much of a simpleton as that. You know there wouldn't be a drop of water in the basket when I got back."

It was the old lady's turn to smile. "Perhaps you are right. But the basket would be a bit cleaner!"

Apart from the sermon, the fellowship of God's saints has a healthy effect. Facing the sun as he approached an Indiana town, a traveler was startled to notice a new stone church with a red neon light flashing, "1-Hour Cleaning." A closer look disclosed that he had been blinded by the sun's glare. The neon sign belonged to a wooden store next to the sanctuary. But does not association with God's people for an hour help remove the spots and stains?

Concerned when a regular attendant stopped coming to services, a minister found the man sitting beside his fireplace. His excuse, "I can get as much out of church staying home. I hear sermons on the radio. Christianity is strictly a personal matter." Without a word the minister took the tongs, lifted a live coal from the fire, placed it off to one side. Then together they watched the glow slowly die out, leaving nothing but a burned-out ember. The man's only comment, "I'll be in church Sunday!"

Joy and peace.—The disciples came to this meeting

gloomy. They mourned the death of their beloved Lord. Though reports had reached them earlier that day that their Master was alive, they came together, as far as they had any certain knowledge, to lament a dead Christ. Then, behold, he appeared in their midst, the living One! No wonder we read, "Then were the disciples glad, when they saw the Lord" (John 20:20).

How often people who are down in the dumps walk into a church service and there receive a new view of Christ's love. They leave rejoicing in a fresh assurance.

Jesus pronounced a benediction on the disciples, "Peace be unto you." Thomas missed both peace and joy. Church attendance does not give joy and peace but provides the instruction and atmosphere to help find a right relationship with Christ, the fountain of both joy and peace.

The commission of Christ.—At this meeting which Thomas missed, the Lord stated that "repentance and remission of sins should be preached in his name among all nations, beginning at Jerusalem." He commissioned them as witnesses: "As my Father hath sent me, even so send I you" (Luke 24:47-48; John 20:21). He gave them a job to do, just as he had done a job for his Heavenly Father.

Every Christian is to confess Christ before men. In the broad sense of the word, we are all missionaries to bear the good news to our circle of relatives, friends, and associates. Sometimes we find this task difficult. Attendance at church should keep this commission before us. People who neglect to meet Christ in worship will have no message to tell others.

8

If Christ Had Not Risen

If Christ be not risen.
—1 Corinthians 15:14

The author will never forget the first funeral service he conducted. A senior at a Bible institute, he was sent out by the Practical Work Department to a funeral parlor in the heart of Chicago. The family was obviously poor and without church affiliation. A twenty-four-year-old mother had died, leaving four children, all too young to understand, and a husband in deep sorrow. But grieving far more demonstrably was the girl's mother. Just as the funeral director was about to close the casket, the mother, leaning over the daughter's face in inconsolable despair, screamed in a loud voice, over and over again, "Never—see—her—again! Never—see—her—again!"

No one sees more frequently than the gospel minister the difference a firm faith in the resurrection of Christ makes in the hour of sorrow. In fact, we little realize how different life would be had Christ not risen from the dead. In his famous resurrection chapter (1 Cor. 15),

Paul begins with an affirmation of Christ's resurrection. After marshaling a list of witnesses he admits that some deny the resurrection of the body. Denial of the resurrection of the body would mean that Christ did not rise, the Christian message would be invalidated, the forgiveness of sins would be nullified, and hope would be obliterated.

No Christian Message

If Christ had not risen from the dead we would have no Christian revelation. The gospel is "Christ died for our sins, was buried, and rose the third day." If untrue, the final supporting beam in the superstructure of the gospel comes tumbling down, crumbling apostolic preaching into worthless ruins.

The theme of almost every sermon in Acts is the resurrection of Christ. The apostles invariably climax their discourses with the glorious fact of Christ's triumph over the tomb. Not a single New Testament writer fails to affirm explicitly or implicitly this truth. The Gospels, the book of Acts, the Epistles, and Revelation all declare him alive after many infallible proofs. If the resurrection be not an actuality then the gospel is evacuated of reality. The Christian message deteriorates into fiction. Faith in a dead Christ avails nothing. Paul spells out this implication, "If Christ be not risen, then is our preaching vain, and your faith is also vain" (1 Cor. 15:14).

In addition, the messengers of the resurrection become false witnesses, not merely mistaken, but prevaricators. What had been palmed off as propagation of truth turns out to be dissemination of a lie. Paul puts it, "Yea, and we are found false witnesses of God; because we have testified of God that he raised up Christ" (v. 15).

From apostolic days to this hour all preaching then has merely been the spreading of a falsehood. Through the years all the great sermons, whether by Peter, Paul, Stephen, Chrysostom, Augustine, Luther, Calvin, Knox, Bunyan, Wesley, Whitefield, Spurgeon, Moody, Truett, or Billy Graham, have been based on error. The thousands of messages heralded every Lord's Day, the great hymns of the church, the sunrise services, the Apostles' Creed all proclaim a fabricated lie.

Were the apostles dishonest men—tricksters, serving worldly interests for their own gain? Was Peter a rascal? Was Paul a knave? Was John a deceiver? Did they adapt their story to court the world's favor and win wealth and fame? They seemed to gain only hatred, pain, and martyrdom. Yet they declared the resurrection because they had seen the risen Christ and knew his resurrection to be true. Their unshaken conviction in his victory over the grave propelled them onward and outward to promulgate a fact that possessed them. What mattered if evil men persecuted to the ultimate? They knew him who had the keys of death, for he had promised, "Because I live, ye shall live also" (John 14:19).

Paul adds, "But now is Christ risen from the dead" (1 Cor. 15:20). Their testimony is reliable. Their message is true. The New Testament is trustworthy.

No Forgiveness of Sins

Leon Tucker relates how Dwight L. Moody sent him to preach in a tent on the north side of Chicago. One night Moody showed up at the meeting when Tucker's text was, "When they were come unto a place called Golgotha . . . they crucified him" (Matt. 27:33-35). He concluded by saying, "Friends, I laid him on the cross tonight. Tomorrow night I will tell you what happened afterwards."

Next day at the workers' conference Moody, spotting Tucker, exclaimed, "Don't go back to your tent any more. I don't need your kind of preaching!"

"What have I done?" asked Tucker. "I preached Christ and him crucified."

"But you left him on the cross last night," Moody replied. "Don't you know a dead Christ never saved anybody? Our sins can't be forgiven apart from a risen Christ. Don't ever preach on that text again without saying, 'God raised him from the dead.' "

The resurrection of Christ certifies God's acceptance of his Son's death on the cross as sufficient atonement for our sin debt. He "was delivered for our offenses, and was raised again for our justification" (Rom. 4:25). The resurrection receipts his payment for our guilt. In some Oriental market places, when the money of the buyer goes down on the table, the hand of the seller goes up to indicate acceptance. Had anything been lacking in the price Jesus paid, he would still be in the tomb. The resurrection indicates the Father's stamp of approval on Christ's redeeming ministry. This is why Paul says, "If Christ be not raised, your faith is vain; ye are yet in your sins."

Many years ago in Detroit, Michigan, Charles Finney preached on the text, "The blood of Jesus Christ, God's

Son, cleanseth us from all sin" (John 1:7). After the service a stranger asked Dr. Finney to walk home with him. Advised against it by church officials who knew the man, Dr. Finney went with the man.

Ushering the preacher into the rear of a building, the stranger locked the door, put the key in his pocket, and said, "Don't be afraid. I'm not going to hurt you. I just want to ask a few questions. Do you believe what you preached tonight?"

Dr. Finney said, "I most certainly do."

The man continued, "We're in the back of a saloon. I'm sole proprietor. Mothers come in here, lay their babies on the counter, and beg me not to sell liquor to their husbands. I turn a deaf ear to their cry. We see to it when a man leaves here he's well under the influence. More than one night a man leaving here has been killed by the express at the tracks. Dr. Finney, tell me, can God forgive a man like me?"

Dr. Finney replied, "I have but one authority, the Word of God which says, 'The blood of Jesus Christ, God's Son, cleanseth us from all sin.' "

"But that's not all," added the man. "In another room we run a gambling hall. If a man doesn't spend all his money on liquor, we bring him back here and with marked cards see to it that he's fleeced out of his last dollar. We send him home penniless to a hungry family. Dr. Finney, I'm sole owner. Tell me honestly, can God forgive a man with a heart like that?"

Again Dr. Finney replied, "I have but one authority, the Word of God which says, 'The blood of Jesus Christ, God's Son, cleanseth us from all sin.' "

The man spoke again. "That's not all. Across the street is my home where live my wife and little daughter. Neither one has had a kind word from me for five years. Their bodies bear marks of my brutal attacks. Dr. Finney, do you think God could forgive a man with a heart like that?"

Dr. Finney's head lowered. His eyes filled with tears as he said, "My friend, you have painted one of the darkest pictures I have ever gazed on, but I still have one authority which says, 'The blood of Jesus Christ cleanseth us from all sin.' "

The man opened the door, ushered the preacher into the night, then never left that room till daybreak—not before ripping up decks of cards and pouring the contents of bottles down the sink. Across the road at home he sat in his living room. His little girl called, "Daddy, Mother says breakfast is ready." When he answered his little girl kindly, she ran back to her mother, "Daddy spoke kind to me! Something is the matter!" The mother followed her little girl to the living room. The man beckoned them both. Taking one on each knee, he explained to their amazement that they had a new husband and daddy. He ended, "I'm done with that business across the street!" The man later became a member, then an official in a leading Detroit church. When asked to tell how his life was changed, he would reply, "The blood of Jesus Christ, God's Son, cleanseth us from all sin."[1]

There's power in the blood—only if Christ rose from the dead! A dead redeemer is no redeemer! But now is Christ risen from the dead. All who have trusted him through the centuries have been released from the penalty of their transgressions. Believers no longer cringe under the terror of a broken law. Jesus paid it all!

No Hope

Apart from Christ's resurrection, what hope do men have? For countless persons life is a meaningless labyrinth filled with boredom, purposelessness, frustration, and futility. Life has been described as the predicament that precedes death, a four-minute mile to the grave, or, a game with some exciting hands to be played before extinction is a common doom. If Christ did not rise, even had we hope in this life, "we would be of all men most miserable" (1 Cor. 15.19).

If death ends all, good works done in love for Christ are to no avail. Our self-denials, our contributions to Christian work, pleasures surrendered to win the favor of the Saviour are all sacrificed in vain. We have let earth go while grasping for a fancied heaven. If Christ rose not, we have no hope of heaven.

A railroad conductor in Suffern, New York, took by mistake some candy heavily dosed with rat poison. He was rushed to the local hospital. The supervising nurse handed him a glass of liquid. When it failed to nauseate him, she gave him a glass of milk containing the whites of six eggs, which he managed to gulp down, but with no results. The nurse had pulled the screen in front of him as she reached for a hypodermic. A doctor rushing in gave him another liquid antidote.

"Doctor," said the conductor, "I don't think these

¹Harry Vom Bruch, *Modern Prodigals and Other Sermons* (Mt. Morris, Ill.: Kable Brothers Co., n.d.), pp. 151-55.

ladies like me. Everything they gave me tastes worse than what they gave me before! This is the first thing that's tasted half decent since I came in!" The doctor looked at the conductor, then started to laugh. The conductor laughed too. The nurse in charge, amazed anyone could laugh while having such a close brush with death, turned to the patient. "Say, weren't you afraid you were going to die?"

Though she phrased her question in the past tense, the conductor knew he wasn't yet out of danger. He answered, "I'm not afraid to die because I know I would go to heaven. If I'd been in heaven ten thousand years already, I wouldn't be any surer of it than I am now! For it's absent from the body and present with the Lord!" Then he added, "I'm looking right straight into the face of death now, and there's no fear!"

The nurse looked at him in astonishment, then put her hand on his shoulder. "You know, I can see in your face that you have no fear of death! Not many who come in here can say that!"

If Christ never rose, there would be no hope of some day possessing perfect, glorified bodies like unto his. No one could have a firm hope of heaven. At every tick of the clock millions suffer pain, whether the pounding of a headache, the sharpness of a toothache, the gnawing of arthritis, the unrelenting pain of cancer. The first begotten from the dead, Christ became the head of a new humanity destined to likewise rise from the dead. As Paul put it, "Christ the firstfruits; afterward they that are Christ's at his coming" (1 Cor. 15.23). Whether lost at sea, absorbed by countless minute organisms, cremated, disintegrated into dust, regardless of the technical problem, the bodies of all believers will some day be raised by the divine power through which God is able to subdue all things unto himself.

Resurrected bodies will be immune to decay; they will be strong, free from disease and death, fitted by the Holy Spirit to live anywhere in the universe—like Christ's body able to go through closed doors or travel with speed in space. All deformities of our present body will be erased. The aches of age, the panting of cardiacs, the languishing of feeble and infirm in old people's homes, nursing homes, and state hospitals will be no more. Instead, our glorified bodies will enjoy eternal youth and vibrant health. As the hymn writer put it,

> No graves on the hillsides of glory,
> For there we shall never more die;
> The old will be young there forever,
> Transformed in a moment of time;
> Immortal we'll stand in His likeness,
> The stars and the sun to outshine.[2]

The grave is no longer an eternal prison for the Christian's body, but just a quiet resting place till the coming of the Lord. No world tragedy, even massive nuclear holocaust, can destroy this hope.

If Christ rose not, no one has hope of ever again seeing loved ones removed by death. Professor Curie, co-discoverer along with his wife of radium, was killed by a carriage in 1906. Mrs. Curie's tragic grief is described

[2]© 1914 and 1942 by Nazarene Publishing House. By permission.

in *The Life of Madame Curie*. She clung to the body. She kissed the face of the corpse time and time again. She wrote to her deceased husband in her diary every day. She wrote, "Your coffin was closed and I could see you no more. We saw you go down into the deep hole. They filled the grave and put flowers on it. Everything is over. It is the end of everything, everything, everything!"[3]

But Christ's resurrection is the guarantee of hope. The dead in Christ have not perished but are with him. Some day there will be glad reunion. We are not of all men most miserable. At Christian funerals tears will flow. But Christians sorrow not as those who have no hope.

A busy, competent physician overworked into a fatal illness. His widow, deeply in love with him, bore up heroically during the funeral. People predicted she would break down when reaction set in. But to the amazement of all, her spirits continued buoyant. One day some friends, calling on her, blurted out, "What's your secret. How have you remained so calm?"

"Come with me to the doctor's waiting room," she answered. Leading them down the hall to his reception room, she snapped on the light, and stood in silence. Suddenly one of the friends saw a sign hanging on a doorknob of the office. Then the others saw it and understood. The widow explained, "The maid forgot to remove that sign. She put all the other rooms in order, but perhaps the Lord let her leave it here. Right after his death I spotted the hand-lettered sign, hanging a little

[3]From Robert Boyd Munger, *What Jesus Says* (Westwood, N. J.: Fleming H. Revell, 1955), p. 128.

unevenly, just as he had left it. That message gave me the courage to go on."

The sign read, "Gone for a little while. Will be with you soon."

> If Easter be not true,
> Then all the lilies low must lie;
> The Flanders poppies fade and die;
> The spring must lose her fairest bloom
> For Christ were still within the tomb—
>   If Easter be not true.
>
> If Easter be not true,
> Then faith must mount on broken wing;
> Then hope no more immortal spring;
> Then hope must lose her mighty urge;
> Life prove a phantom, death a dirge—
>   If Easter be not true.
>
> If Easter be not true,
> 'Twere foolishness the cross to bear;
> He died in vain who suffered there;
> What matter though we laugh or cry,
> Be good or evil, live or die,
>   If Easter be not true?
>
> If Easter be not true—
> But it is true, and Christ is risen!
> And mortal spirit from its prison
> Of sin and death with him may rise!
> Worthwhile the struggle, sure the prize,
>   Since Easter, aye, is true![4]

[4]Henry Barstow, from *Masterpieces of Religious Verse*. Reprinted by permission of Harper & Row, Publishers.